INSIGHT'S

BIBLE APPLICATION GUIDE
Isaiah – Malachi

A LIFE LESSON FROM EVERY CHAPTER

From the Bible-Teaching Ministry of
CHARLES R. SWINDOLL

Insight's Bible Application Guide: Isaiah–Malachi
A Life Lesson from Every Chapter
From the Bible-Teaching Ministry of Charles R. Swindoll

Charles R. Swindoll has devoted his life to the accurate, practical teaching and application of God's Wo
and His grace. A pastor at heart, Chuck has served as senior pastor to congregations in Texas, Massachuse
and California. Since 1998, he has served as senior pastor-teacher of Stonebriar Commun
Church in Frisco, Texas, but Chuck's listening audience extends far beyond a local church body. As a lead
program in Christian broadcasting since 1979, *Insight for Living* airs in major Christian radio markets arou
the world, reaching people groups in languages they can understand. Chuck's extensive writing minis
has also served the body of Christ worldwide and his leadership as president and now chancellor of Dal
Theological Seminary has helped prepare and equip a new generation of men and women for minis
Chuck and Cynthia, his partner in life and ministry, have four grown children, ten grandchildren, and fo
great-grandchildren.

Published By: IFL Publishing House, A Division of Insight for Living Ministries
Post Office Box 5000, Frisco, Texas 75034-0055

Editor in Chief: Cynthia Swindoll, President, Insight for Living Ministries
Executive Vice President: Wayne Stiles, Th.M., D.Min., Dallas Theological Seminary
Writers: Malia Rodriguez, Th.M., Dallas Theological Seminary
    Sharifa Stevens, Th.M., Dallas Theological Seminary
    Wayne Stiles, Th.M., D.Min., Dallas Theological Seminary
Substantive Editor: Jim Craft, M.A., English, Mississippi College; Certificate of Biblical and Theologica
Studies, Dallas Theological Seminary
Copy Editor: Paula McCoy, B.A., English, Texas A&M University-Commerce
Project Supervisor, Creative Ministries: Megan Meckstroth, B.S., Advertising, University of Florida
Project Coordinator, Publishing: Jana Waller, B.A., Communications Studies, Baylor University
Proofreader: LeeAnna Swartz, B.A., Communications, Moody Bible Institute
Designer: Margaret Gulliford, B.A., Graphic Design, Taylor University
Production Artist: Nancy Gustine, B.F.A., Advertising Art, University of North Texas

ISBN: 978-1-57972-969-1
Printed in the United States of America

Table of Contents

A Letter from Chuck

If you have ever found yourself asking, "Why won't God *speak*?" you will *love* reading through the Prophetic Books of the Old Testament. Repeatedly, the prophets picked up their quills and scratched out these words: "This is what the LORD says. . . ."

You want to know the mind of God? You want to know if God is true to His word? *Read the books of the prophets.* These aren't words soaked in formaldehyde. They aren't historical relics without relevance for today. They are alive! Each is filled with hope, holiness, justice, and mercy, teaching us truths we desperately need in our world this very day.

My hope is that *Insight's Bible Application Guide: Isaiah – Malachi* will help you gain a new appreciation for God's grace. By boiling down every single chapter of the prophets to one paragraph of application each, this volume allows the message of the Prophetic Books to take hold of your everyday life. God's gracious refrain in each prophetic song can be summarized in Ezekiel's simple words: "I don't want you to die, says the Sovereign LORD. Turn back and live!" (Ezekiel 18:32 NLT).

Our goal in providing you this volume is to make the sometimes intimidating Prophetic Books accessible and useful. As you study Isaiah, rejoice in the once-and-for-all sacrifice of the Suffering Servant, who atoned for a sin-sick world. While reading about the tragedy of idolatry in Ezekiel, take heart that God can make even dry bones live. Find hope while reading the book of Joel, that God will restore the years marked with calamity.

If you need an extra measure of God's grace in your relationship with Him, know that the Old Testament prophecies repeatedly proclaim that God remained ready to extend grace and show mercy to those who repented and returned to Him. The Lord is still waiting. He's waiting to welcome you back — no matter how long you've been gone or where you've been.

I'm confident that the volume you hold in your hand will show you how to apply the principles behind the prophets' exhortations to your life.

Charles R. Swindoll

About the Writers

Malia Rodriguez

Malia received her master of theology degree in Systematic Theology from Dallas Theological Seminary. She now serves as a writer in the Creative Ministries Department of Insight for Living Ministries, where she is able to merge her love of theology with her gift for words. Malia and her husband, Matt, who is also a graduate of Dallas Theological Seminary, live in the Dallas area with their son and daughter. Malia contributed the chapters on Jeremiah, Daniel, Hosea, and Malachi.

Sharifa Stevens

A New York native, Sharifa earned a bachelor of arts degree from Columbia University before moving to Dallas, Texas, where she received a master of theology degree from Dallas Theological Seminary. She currently serves as a writer for the Creative Ministries Department of Insight for Living Ministries. Sharifa is passionate about worship through music and the intersection of faith and culture. She is wife to a Renaissance man and mother to two lively boys. Sharifa contributed the chapters on Isaiah, Ezekiel, Joel, Amos, Jonah, Michah, Zephaniah, and Zechariah.

Wayne Stiles

Wayne received his master of theology in Pastoral Ministries and doctor of ministry in Biblical Geography from Dallas Theological Seminary. In 2005, after serving in the pastorate for fourteen years, Wayne joined the staff at Insight for Living Ministries, where he leads and labors alongside a team of writers, editors, and pastors as the executive vice president and chief content officer. Wayne and his wife, Cathy, live in Aubrey, Texas, and have two daughters in college. Wayne contributed the chapters on Lamentations, Obadiah, Nahum, Habakkuk, and Haggai.

What Is the Value of the Prophetic Books Today?

Images of violence, destruction, and wrath fill the prophetic pages of the Bible. We can't help but feel the weight of sin and sadness as we wait with Isaiah for the Assyrian invasion, or walk with Jeremiah through the devastated streets of Jerusalem, or observe with Ezekiel God's glory departing the temple. And in the Minor Prophets, we find more of the same theme: judgment, more judgment, and even more judgment.

Hopelessness seems to riddle the depressing landscape of the prophets . . . or does it?

Though we might feel we have to read the Prophetic Books of the Bible with a box of tissues in hand, we don't. Why? Because *hope*—not hopelessness—forms the foundation of Isaiah through Malachi. We see in these books that God destroyed in order to discipline His sinful children for the purpose of drawing them closer to Him. We also see that He rebuilt what He destroyed (Jeremiah 33:7).

This facet of God remains true today. His discipline leads to spiritual renewal and abundant life (Isaiah 38:16; Hebrews 12:11). As we walk through difficult times, the prophets can help us hope for a future time when everyone will put down their weapons and true worship will fill the earth.

The prophets teach us three of God's attributes: His justice, His grace, and His sovereignty. Because God is righteous, He will not tolerate sin. Therefore, His all-consuming justice must punish people for their wickedness. But God's purpose for disciplining His people is always restoration.

The prophets portray God's justice, but they also remind us of God's faithfulness. He made an everlasting covenant with Israel (Genesis 12:1–3) and gave them the Mosaic Law so that they would stand out as God's chosen people among the nations (Deuteronomy 14:2). But God's people followed neighboring nations into various forms of disobedience. God proved His grace by sending prophet after prophet, who faithfully called His people to repentance. God sent Isaiah to tell His people about the coming Servant—the Messiah, Jesus Christ—who would once and for all pay for their sin and rule with righteousness (Isaiah 9:6; 53:4–6). The Lord sent Daniel to give Israel a glimpse of the future and of God's sovereign control over all the kingdoms on earth (Daniel 4:34–35). God sent Malachi to rebuke the religious leaders for leading the people astray (Malachi 2:1–9), but He also promised to send the perfect King-Priest to lead His people (Zechariah 6:12–13).

God's grace draws people to Him and away from idolatry, greed, and injustice. But even if people don't repent and God's wrath comes down, hope still emerges through the rubble. While sin hardens the soil of our hearts, making us unreceptive to God's Spirit, judgment tills the soil, causes pain, and reveals our desperate need for the Lord.

The flip side of destruction is restoration. We all have experienced the pain caused by our own sin and by the wicked actions of others. The Prophetic Books in the Bible can help us trust in God's sovereignty, justice, and grace in the midst of agony. The Lord spoke through His prophets in order to prepare people for the coming Messiah, in whom we have hope (Hebrews 1:1–2). Jesus carried the weight of our sins on His shoulders—when He died on the cross—and He rose from the dead so that hope could pierce the bleakness of sin and death in our lives. And when Christ returns, He will destroy sin, pain, and death. The pain of the prophets will be behind us, and the grace they looked forward to will envelop us for eternity.

The hope of the prophets points us to that magnificent future.

INSIGHT'S
BIBLE APPLICATION GUIDE
Isaiah – Malachi

Isaiah

Isaiah 1

Zion will be redeemed with justice
And her repentant ones with righteousness.
But transgressors and sinners will be crushed together,
And those who forsake the LORD will come to an end.
— *Isaiah 1:27–28*

In Hebrew, *Isaiah* means "the Lord saves." Isaiah's prophecies—and really, all the Prophetic Books—can be summed up by Isaiah 1:27–28: *God will bring redemption and justice to repentant people and destruction to those who forsake Him.* Justice and righteousness pair together in the passage, because justice is a natural outworking of a humble heart. Crushing sinners is the ultimate righteous judgment delivered by the Lord Himself in response to injustice, idolatry, and arrogance. The difference between righteous people and sinners is not the absence of sin but whom they trust for deliverance. The repentant live by faith in God; the arrogant live only for themselves. Pride separates the repentant sinner from the arrogant one. At the crucifixion, two thieves suffered alongside Jesus: one repented of his sin while the other held on to his pride to the last. Only one thief was with Jesus in Paradise. Isaiah points us to humility.

Isaiah 2

Stop regarding man, whose breath of life is in his nostrils;
For why should he be esteemed?　　　— *Isaiah 2:22*

On a walk in midtown Manhattan, we'd be hard-pressed to see a swath of uninterrupted sky. Instead, tall buildings poke through the daylight, competing to reach the clouds. The city skyline is an impressive work of humanity, a symbol of affluence and bold-ness. Yet, in Isaiah's prophecy about the last days, the best that *humanity* can offer will crumble in the face of God's majestic judg-ment. In the day when the Lord will dwell on His holy mountain, people will squeeze into the darkest caverns to hide. God's awe-someness will overwhelm. The God of the last days is the God of today. Don't be fooled by human-made attempts to attain the heavens — they didn't work for the people of Babel (Genesis 11). It won't work for us to chase glory by our own means. Instead, we can give the glory to whom it belongs — our King.

Isaiah 3

*Moreover, the L*ORD *said, "Because the daughters of Zion are proud*
And walk with heads held high and seductive eyes,
And go along with mincing steps
And tinkle the bangles on their feet,
Therefore the Lord will afflict the scalp of the daughters of Zion with
    scabs,
*And the L*ORD *will make their foreheads bare."*   — *Isaiah 3:16–17*

The "daughters of Zion" were a synecdoche (a term signifying when a part is used to signify the whole) of the people of Judah. Their pride led to greed, to taking advantage of the poor, and to displaying conspicuous consumption. Captivity and exile would reckon with Judah's humility deficit. God is not impressed with stuff — He gives every good gift, after all. When the acquisition of stuff replaces honor to God, it is idolatry. God exalts those hum-ble enough to praise the Giver instead of the gifts. In Luke 18, Jesus shared a parable with His audience about the prayers of a contrite tax collector and a proud Pharisee. Jesus stated that the tax collector—whose prayer was simply, "God, be merciful to me, the sinner!"—was justified because "everyone who exalts himself will be humbled, but he who humbles himself will be exalted" (Luke 18:13–14).

Isaiah 4

In that day the Branch of the LORD will be beautiful and glorious, and the fruit of the earth will be the pride and the adornment of the survivors of Israel.   *—Isaiah 4:2*

Just as Isaiah 4:2 does, so also Zechariah 6:12 speaks of a man named Branch. This one will sprout up and rebuild the temple of the Lord. Isaiah also used this term in 11:1 to describe Messiah. In the millennium, Jesus Christ will return to the earth to rule, and the righteous remnant of Israel will finally know Him as Messiah. The tone of Isaiah 4 is hopeful, describing God's tangible presence ruling over a people who are reconciled to Him. God graciously paused between judgment prophecies to deliver to His people a message of hope. He guaranteed them a forthcoming time of restoration, confirming that Israel would not be utterly destroyed. He offered an opportunity for Israel to repent, but they didn't. Who knows what would have occurred if Israel had repented? God's offer to Israel and the world stands even now: if we believe in Jesus, the Branch, our eternal future in heaven is secure. If we do not accept Jesus' offer of salvation, an eternal future in hell is certain. His mercy can triumph over our judgment.

Isaiah 5

Their banquets are accompanied by lyre and harp, by tambourine
*   and flute, and by wine;*
But they do not pay attention to the deeds of the LORD,
Nor do they consider the work of His hands.   —Isaiah 5:12*

The people of Israel produced the sour grapes of bloodshed and distress (Isaiah 5:2, 7) because they were disconnected from their Source—God. Our lives hum and tweet with cell phone notifications, the tap-tap-tap of typing, deafening screeches of construction vehicles, the whizz of jet engines, chants of subways, and barks of car horns. Even our relaxation time chatters with buzzes and whirrs. All this clatter fills our ears and can dull our spiritual senses. A few moments of idle time can become *idol* time when it steals our attention from the things of God. Sometimes we require the hush, pause, and Sabbath rest in order to settle our minds on God's Word, to pray with purpose and without distraction, and to worship the Lord with our undivided attention. We are the branches of God's vineyard—we must stay connected to Him in order to thrive.

Isaiah 6

In the year of King Uzziah's death I saw the Lord sitting on a throne,
lofty and exalted, with the train of His robe filling the temple.
Seraphim stood above Him, each having six wings: with two he cov-
ered his face, and with two he covered his feet, and with two he flew.
And one called out to another and said,
"Holy, Holy, Holy, is the LORD of hosts,
The whole earth is full of His glory."   —Isaiah 6:1–3*

Isaiah met with the Lord of Hosts and witnessed His glory and holiness. Isaiah's response? Conviction, exposure, and woe

(Isaiah 6:5). In the bright light of God's presence, the sin of humanity is instantly exposed. But the Lord's light was not meant to shame Isaiah. Instead, the light made Isaiah aware of what God already knew: there's a great gulf between God's holiness and even the most righteous person's ways. God did not leave Isaiah in his woe; instead, He provided Isaiah with hot coals to cleanse his lips, which qualified Isaiah to speak. God then gave him a calling as a prophet. And so our Holy God cleanses and qualifies every Christian, equipping us to be His witnesses (Acts 1:8) regardless of our pedigree or worthiness. Our past doesn't dictate our fitness to be God's witness. If we confess our sins, God is faithful to forgive and cleanse us (1 John 1:9).

Isaiah 7

Then the Lord spoke again to Ahaz, saying, "Ask a sign for yourself from the Lord your God; make it deep as Sheol or high as heaven." But Ahaz said, "I will not ask, nor will I test the Lord!" Then he said, "Listen now, O house of David! Is it too slight a thing for you to try the patience of men, that you will try the patience of my God as well?"   —Isaiah 7:10–13

Isaiah was commissioned by God to prophesy to people who heard yet didn't understand the word of the Lord (Isaiah 6:9). In Isaiah 7, King Ahaz of Judah evidenced this spiritual deafness. He was afraid because the king of Israel had partnered with Aram's king in order to invade Judah's capital city Jerusalem. The Lord of Hosts assured Ahaz that rival kings would not overtake Judah. The Lord offered assurance to Ahaz and even spoke in close terms with him, saying, "Ask a sign for yourself from the Lord *your* God" (Isaiah 7:11, emphasis added). But Ahaz, with empty modesty, rejected the Lord's assurance — he had already planned a counteralliance with Assyria. How ironic that Ahaz used a biblical concept — likely quoting Deuteronomy 6:16 — to refuse dependence on God. How many of us have been guilty of false piety, faithlessness, and self-reliance? Our knowledge of God and the Bible is worthless if it's not founded in faith and dependence.

Isaiah 8

"You are not to say, 'It is a conspiracy!'
In regard to all that this people call a conspiracy,
And you are not to fear what they fear or be in dread of it.
"It is the LORD *of hosts whom you should regard as holy.*
And He shall be your fear,
And He shall be your dread." —*Isaiah 8:12–13*

In Isaiah 7, God gave Ahaz a sign of Judah's safety: a woman would give birth to a son and name him Immanuel (Isaiah 7:14) — this was also a foreshadowing of Jesus' birth. In chapter 8, Isaiah's wife delivered a baby, Maher-shalal-hash-baz (translated, "quick to plunder, swift to spoil"), as a sign of Assyria's victory over Israel and Aram. Swirling in all of these promises, though, was the imminent threat of war on three sides. This terror naturally fueled paranoia and conspiracies. God adjured Isaiah to take no part in conspiracies, because God alone controls kingdoms and outcomes. We live in trying times even now, fraught with social and political rumor — but God is with us. What was true for Isaiah is true for us: we must trust in Immanuel, living out His words in Matthew 10:28: "Do not fear those who kill the body but are unable to kill the soul; but rather fear Him who is able to destroy both soul and body in hell."

Isaiah 9

For a child will be born to us, a son will be given to us;
And the government will rest on His shoulders;
And His name will be called Wonderful Counselor, Mighty God,
Eternal Father, Prince of Peace. —Isaiah 9:6

Isaiah described Messiah with a poetic air of joy. Though the people of Israel walked in darkness and would receive God's unwavering punishment (Isaiah 9:12, 17, 21), the zeal of the Lord of Hosts favors the throne of David. There will be peace and prosperity one day through the Prince of Peace. Along with this joyful description of Messiah are messages of woe. How could Isaiah communicate such joy in the midst of such deep darkness? Isaiah was a man submitted both to God's judgment and mercy. He had witnessed God's holiness and was transformed (6:6). He had seen God stretch out His hand to offer protection (7:11) and would trust Him to stretch out His hand to punish. When we worship and follow Jesus, we're not instantly removed from our fallen world. We're still surrounded by darkness. But with Jesus, we have the Light to lead us (John 8:12), we are called to walk in the Light (Isaiah 2:5; 1 John 1:7), and we are to point others to it.

Isaiah 10

Is the axe to boast itself over the one who chops with it?
Is the saw to exalt itself over the one who wields it?
That would be like a club wielding those who lift it,
Or like a rod lifting him who is not wood. —Isaiah 10:15

Who would dare share bragging rights with the Lord? Who would take credit for the things He has done? Yet Assyria, the chastening tool in the hand of the Holy One of Israel, did just that: it claimed for itself the glory for its victories (Isaiah 10:5–8). Because of this, God set His sights on punishing the arrogance of Assyria (10:12) . . . but only after the Assyrians had completed His work in Jerusalem. The Israelites *did* know God, unlike the Assyrians, and yet had the gall to perpetually worship idols and fail to acknowledge Him. God promised to tear down every idol in both Samaria and Jerusalem (10:11). Failing to acknowledge God is not unique to Israel. It's a product of sin — a chronic disease of humanity, even God's people — to attribute our possessions, wealth, and favor to ourselves rather than to God. People of God must strive to relinquish false bragging rights by boasting only in the Lord (Psalm 20:7).

Isaiah 11

And the wolf will dwell with the lamb,
And the leopard will lie down with the young goat,
And the calf and the young lion and the fatling together;
And a little boy will lead them.   —*Isaiah 11:6*

The world Isaiah lived in was marked by stark contrasts in standards of living. The wealthy continued to expand their profits through immoral means; they exploited their neighbors and inflated prices for goods. Justice was a commodity that could be bought and sold, and the poor could not afford it. Imagine the relief that washed over the Israelites when they heard about the "shoot of Jesse" (Isaiah 11:1, 10) who would rule impartially in a kingdom where the most vulnerable — children — would be safe from harm! In a world where the unborn are in peril, where the chasm deepens between the haves and have-nots, where morality is eroding, Isaiah's message still resonates. The world's predatory standard is not God's standard. In the future, He will raise up a standard through Jesus Christ, and every people and nation will submit to it. And there will be peace. Until then, we can model a peace in our relationships that points to Him.

Isaiah 12

"Behold, God is my salvation,
I will trust and not be afraid;
For the LORD GOD is my strength and song,
And He has become my salvation." — *Isaiah 12:2*

Have you ever been positively overwhelmed by an experience — the birth of a healthy baby, witnessing a captivating sunrise, pitching the perfect game, sinking your teeth into a succulent rib-eye? The joy that bubbles up on these happy occasions is mere foreshadowing for the praise that our God commands. God's majesty, God's compassion, God's holiness is so awe-inspiring that it compels His people to praise Him. Isaiah wrote of the praise that would pour from the people's lips as they contemplated the life of peace they would experience because of the righteous rule of God and because of their salvation. When we think about what the Lord, through the sacrifice of His Son, Jesus, has saved us from — despair in death, separation from God, unforgiveness, slavery to sin — how can we help but declare that the Lord God is our strength, our song, and our salvation? God's goodness is a gift we just can't keep to ourselves (Psalm 51:14 – 15).

Isaiah 13

Anyone who is found will be thrust through,
And anyone who is captured will fall by the sword.
Their little ones also will be dashed to pieces
Before their eyes;
Their houses will be plundered
And their wives ravished. —*Isaiah 13:15–16*

Isaiah delivered an oracle of reckoning to Babylon in chapter 13: God's recompense for wickedness. Babylon had represented humanity's hubris since Genesis 11, when the people of Babel (another name for Babylon) sought to build a tower to reach the heavens on their own strength. God opposes the proud, and here in Isaiah, His opposition comes with annihilation. Perhaps most disturbing in this passage is the promise that even women and children—noncombatants and the most vulnerable—would experience gruesome deaths. Is God the agent of this? No! In His mercy, God had restrained opposing regimes from carrying out the full brunt of their barbarism. But the Babylonians had systematically made their stand against God, and He gave them over to the results of their pride. (See Romans 1:24–25.) The godless Babylonian men put everyone under their authority in jeopardy. *Everyone.* It's sobering to know that our spiritual choices aren't made in a vacuum. Our sin can imperil not only us but also those closest to us. Likewise, our faith and obedience to God can bless our entire household. Choose wisely.

Isaiah 14

"The LORD has broken the staff of the wicked,
The scepter of rulers
Which used to strike the peoples in fury with unceasing strokes,
Which subdued the nations in anger with unrestrained persecution.
The whole earth is at rest and is quiet;
They break forth into shouts of joy."   *—Isaiah 14:5–7*

When justice is meted out, observers breathe a sigh of relief, victims experience rest and safety, and perpetrators receive their deserved punishment. In the future, when Babylon's king falls, the earth—from the peaceable nation of Israel (Isaiah 14:3) to the natural world itself (14:8)—will exhale in relief, finally free from haughty oppression and domination. Even more important than the relief of the earth is the object lesson that those who attempt to make themselves like the Most High will ultimately find themselves hurtling toward Sheol (14:14–15). The sins of idolatry and narcissism lead to certain punishment, because the Lord does not share His glory with anyone (42:8). Isaiah used Babylon's own mythology in his prophecy condemning Babylon. The phrases "above the stars of God" and "the recesses of the north" (14:13) depict where Babylon's pagan gods were revered. The false gods, along with the Babylonian kingdom, would descend to join the dead in anonymous indignity. In the future, God will completely hush the warmongering and prideful. Until then, we can emulate Him by living with compassion, defending justice, and practicing fairness.

Isaiah 15

My heart cries out for Moab;
His fugitives are as far as Zoar and Eglath-shelishiyah,
For they go up the ascent of Luhith weeping;
Surely on the road to Horonaim they raise a cry of distress over
their ruin.　　　　　　　　　　　　　*—Isaiah 15:5*

In Isaiah 15:5 (and also Isaiah 16:9), the prophet Isaiah expressed sympathy for the plight of Moab's residents who would scatter in a desperate attempt to seek safety from foreign invasion. Compared to the unabashed taunting of the Babylonian king in the previous chapter, this verse stands out in its pity. The chapter ends with the continued ravaging of the region (15:9), but what does this "heart cry" from the prophet and from God by extension mean? Perhaps Jesus' thoughts in Matthew 9:36 can further explain: "Seeing the people, He felt compassion for them, because they were distressed and dispirited like sheep without a shepherd." Could it be that God saw the distress of His errant sheep? Or perhaps these displaced people reminded Him of Ruth the Moabitess (Ruth 1:4), the great-grandmother of David (4:17) whose kingdom God swore to uphold. Some mistake the world's woes as God's capricious wrath. The truth is when we experience suffering, God is grieved too. He does not rejoice over the destruction of others—neither should we.

Isaiah 16

Send the tribute lamb to the ruler of the land,
From Sela by way of the wilderness to the mountain of the daughter of Zion.
Then, like fleeing birds or scattered nestlings,
The daughters of Moab will be at the fords of the Arnon.
　　　　　　　　　　　　　—Isaiah 16:1–2

The Arnon was a northern river boundary separating Moab from Israel. Isaiah contrasted the needy, worried Moabite women of his day with the future daughters of Zion. During the forthcoming millennium, Israel will be free of corruption, and a faithful Judge will sit in the tent of David (Isaiah 16:5) and grant refuge to Moab. And during the prophet's present day, he also warned Moab of impending punishment for its pride (16:13–14). With startling specificity, Isaiah told the people of Moab that God would grant them three years until their destruction. In spite of Isaiah's specific prophecy, Moab continued to entreat false gods (16:12) and so sealed its fate. Isaiah steadfastly warned those in his hearing that pride through idolatry or arrogance leads to punishment by God. Imbedded in the warning, though, was the promise of peace through dependence on and worship of the Holy One. How can *we* have peace with God? Flee from pride. Do justice, love kindness, and walk humbly with God (Micah 6:8).

Isaiah 17

In that day their strong cities will be like forsaken places in the forest,
Or like branches which they abandoned before the sons of Israel;
And the land will be a desolation.   *—Isaiah 17:9*

Imagine defending modern-day slavery in our country as a shrewd business and an institution blessed by God. Now, none but the most extreme would consider reinstating slavery in the United States, but it was once a popular practice. Likewise, in Isaiah 7, King Ahaz trusted political popular opinion for prosperity rather than God. Isaiah counseled King Ahaz to trust in the Lord and not fear the brewing coalition between the kings of Aram and Israel. In chapter 17, God revealed more about why they were about to be snuffed out: Judah believed the nations were numerous and powerful (Isaiah 17:12). Just because a cause is favorable to the majority does not make it a just or good cause; it just makes it popular. Believers must regularly run ideas through the trusted foundation of Scripture and the work of God. Fads fade, but God's Word stands forever.

Isaiah 18

At that time a gift of homage will be brought to the LORD of hosts
From a people tall and smooth,
Even from a people feared far and wide,
A powerful and oppressive nation,
Whose land the rivers divide—
To the place of the name of the LORD of hosts, even Mount Zion.
—Isaiah 18:7

The earth is the Lord's footstool (Isaiah 66:1), and all the kingdoms of the earth will ultimately submit to Him. Chapter 18 continued the oracles from God against foreign nations. Ethiopia, also known as Cush, was warned by Isaiah's prophecy that the Lord was quietly watching the nation as a farmer waits for harvest, only to pluck and prune it before it fully flowered. Even then, Ethiopia would not be utterly destroyed. Isaiah predicted that in the last days the Lord will receive tribute from this fearsome nation. We as believers cannot count out any individual or any particular country from submission and relationship with the Lord. God has the ability and the compassion to prune a life for His glory. We can be reassured that the Lord is intently aware of even the most corrupt nations and will not fail to act in His perfect timing.

Isaiah 19

The LORD will strike Egypt, striking but healing; so they will return to the LORD, and He will respond to them and will heal them.

—*Isaiah 19:22*

Though Egypt was a major power during Isaiah's day, the nation was under God's chastening hand and couldn't save itself. Isaiah prophesied concerning Egypt's impotence even in the areas of its established strength: wisdom, agriculture, and military might. Egypt's strengths would come to nothing in the day of reckoning. However, in the eschatological future, the Lord will show Egypt favor. Egypt, a polytheistic nation, will have only one altar—to the one, true God. Isaiah prophesied something that would make the ears of every Israelite tingle in disbelief: a day when *Egypt* will know the Lord and cry out to God in the same way the Israelites did when they were oppressed by Egypt before the exodus. God's desire is reconciliation and healing, even for our most bitter enemies. Our present adversaries could be our future co-heirs in blessing—this should lead us to pray for them with hope and compassion.

Isaiah 20

At that time the LORD spoke through Isaiah the son of Amoz, saying, "Go and loosen the sackcloth from your hips and take your shoes off your feet." And he did so, going naked and barefoot.   —*Isaiah 20:2*

At the command of God, for three years, Isaiah wore only under-garments in order to typify the shaming of Egypt and Cush because of Assyrian domination (a prophecy fulfilled in 701 BC). The prophet demonstrated not only the fate of the Egyptians and

Cushites but also his willingness to fully submit to whatever the Lord required of him. Isaiah was not given permission to explain his actions for three long years. He must have endured mockery, discomfort, and perhaps even sickness due to exposure. To add to this, his message was unbelievable to the people because Egypt and Cush were such superpowers. How could *these nations* be enslaved to anyone? There may be a time where the Lord will call us outside of our comfort zones to be witnesses to His truth. May we be as brave as Isaiah in trusting and obeying God, even when we are at odds with popular culture.

Isaiah 21

O my threshed people, and my afflicted of the threshing floor!
What I have heard from the LORD of hosts,
The God of Israel, I make known to you. —Isaiah 21:10

Both in times of war and peace, a watchman—think of a security guard—looks out for the first signs of danger in order to alert the people under his care. In this chapter, several watchmen had grim news; Babylon would surely fall (Isaiah 21:9), Edom would have a long night of siege with little relief (21:13), and Arabia would produce fugitives (21:14). For the people of Judah and even Judah's enemies, Isaiah was appointed as the watchman. God was gracious enough to announce warning before calamity hit, to provide His people and even their enemies time to turn and repent. Sadly, God foretold the people's indifference from the very beginning (6:9–10). A watchman can only watch and warn; it's up to the people to act. The same is true today—we share the gospel and tell others of God's desire for repentance, but we cannot save souls. It's up to the mercy of God and the will of each person to respond.

Isaiah 22

"What right do you have here,
And whom do you have here,
That you have hewn a tomb for yourself here,
You who hew a tomb on the height,
You who carve a resting place for yourself in the rock?"

— *Isaiah 22:16*

Isaiah deftly contrasted Shebna and Eliakim and the people of Judah by examining where they placed their trust. Shebna, a steward of the kingdom, should have been warning the people about God's wrath; instead, he constructed an elaborate memorial tomb for himself! Because he was more concerned about his name than God's, God had him die anonymously in poverty in a foreign land. God would replace Shebna with Eliakim—but Eliakim would ultimately crumble under the weight of the Judeans' expectations because they consulted him instead of consulting God. No leader, no matter how learned, can replace God's counsel. We must vet advice and leadership with God's Word—whether in politics, relationships, or spiritual and money matters. Instead of blindly following, we then can submit to leadership with realistic expectations. The Lord bears our burdens, changes our circumstances, protects and shields us, and provides for us. People can—and should—serve God by leading and counseling others, but we are incapable of taking His place.

Isaiah 23

Who has planned this against Tyre, the bestower of crowns,
Whose merchants were princes, whose traders were the honored of
*   the earth?*
The LORD of hosts has planned it, to defile the pride of all beauty,
To despise all the honored of the earth. —*Isaiah 23:8–9*

God's sovereignty crossed the deserts of Babylon and entered into
the realm of the seas with the oracle against Tyre—a maritime
metropolis of far-reaching influence (Isaiah 23:3–5). The self-
importance of the country could not stand against the power of
God, and He likened the besieged Tyre to a virgin who was robbed
of her innocence and beauty in the most violent way (23:12). For
Isaiah's audience, hearing about the fall of Tyre would be more
shocking than watching the World Trade Center—that grand
structure symbolizing the powerful commerce and ability of the
region—crumble on September 11, 2001. It's hard for us to
imagine seemingly impregnable symbols of wealth reduced to
rubble. Our frailty, our finiteness, is sure—no matter the measure of our wealth and power. Because of sin, we are all subject
to futility and death. Through God, let us be steadfast against the
dark forces of this world.

Isaiah 24

The earth will be completely laid waste and completely despoiled, for
the LORD has spoken this word. —*Isaiah 24:3*

The oracles of God had been directed to Israel and to the surrounding nations, but in Isaiah 24, His judgment extended to
the entire globe in language that recalls—and reverses—the
creation themes of Genesis 1. Just as "God said, let there be . . ."

and good creation came into existence, in the last days, the earth will be laid waste at the word of the Lord. The human-made hierarchies that exist between master and slave, mistress and servant, creditor and debtor will be erased in equal-opportunity annihilation. Only One has the authority to create order and bestow importance, but His creation failed to submit to it. The sin of pride affected not only humanity but cursed the whole of creation. The Lord punishes in the last days, but thankfully, He also promises to restore (Isaiah 11:10)—including a new heaven and a new earth (Revelation 21:1). Such truth about the future should cause us to live with humility and submission toward God.

Isaiah 25

He will swallow up death for all time,
And the Lord GOD will wipe tears away from all faces,
And He will remove the reproach of His people from all the earth;
For the LORD has spoken.
And it will be said in that day,
"Behold, this is our God for whom we have waited that He might
*   save us.*
This is the LORD for whom we have waited;
Let us rejoice and be glad in His salvation."   —Isaiah 25:8 – 9

The Lord has hardwired us to commemorate treasured times with our senses—the psalmist even said "O *taste* and *see* that the LORD is good" (Psalm 34:8, emphasis added). God had the Israelites taste the bitter herbs and unleavened bread, hear the bleating of sacrificial lambs, and see the blood drip from their doorposts during Passover. And when salvation is fulfilled, tears are dried, and death is dead, God will throw a gala unlike any we've ever seen, tasted, or heard (Luke 22:18). Some of life's most joyous occasions are celebrated with feasting: Christmas, Thanksgiving, weddings, birthdays . . . even Super Bowl Sunday. Just like the father of the prodigal son killed the fattened calf because his beloved had returned to him (Luke 15:22–23), our Father has waited for His people to say yes to total dependence and reliance on Him. When that day comes . . . heaven and earth will hardly contain the joy. In faith and hope we can rejoice today.

Isaiah 26

Though the wicked is shown favor,
He does not learn righteousness;
He deals unjustly in the land of uprightness,
And does not perceive the majesty of the LORD.　　—Isaiah 26:10

"That's not fair!" How many times have we responded indignantly to getting a speeding ticket, being grounded, or receiving a bad grade? Though we live in a fallen world rippling with the aftershocks of sin, many times we actually *deserve* what we get—or worse. We tend to see ourselves in the most merciful light and reserve cold, hard justice for our enemies. Thankfully, God's perspective is more holy. He sees through the eternal lens of perfection, justice, and mercy. Because God looks at the heart, humanity is no mystery to God—He knows who will receive His grace and who is unrepentant in wickedness. We may hear people complaining about the restrictive nature of the gospel with statements such as, "Why would only those who believe in Jesus receive eternal life? That's not fair!" Our response as believers? Share the gospel with others. Confess that we don't always know God's will. Encourage others that God knows the heart (1 Samuel 16:7) even when we don't.

Isaiah 27

"Or let him rely on My protection,
Let him make peace with Me,
Let him make peace with Me." —Isaiah 27:5

God is Creator, Vinedresser, Cultivator. He takes no joy in death. In this chapter, God referred to Israel as a vine that He lovingly tends. Without wrath, He would fight Israel's enemies — represented by thorns and briars (Isaiah 27:4). Even better, the thorns and thistles could submit themselves to God, and there would be peace. Translated literally from Hebrew, Isaiah 27:5 reads, *"With me, let them make peace,"* to emphasize both the lovingkindness and generosity of God in extending the opportunity of peace even to Israel's enemies and also to reveal Himself as the Source of lasting peace. In our outreach to people, we have the opportunity to tell of God's desire to give them peace, to cultivate and tend to their lives, to make them fruitful. Let's enthusiastically share what makes the good news so good — through Jesus, God has made a way through the thorns of sin and death to peace.

Isaiah 28

Woe to the proud crown of the drunkards of Ephraim,
And to the fading flower of its glorious beauty,
Which is at the head of the fertile valley
Of those who are overcome with wine! —Isaiah 28:1

One would *have* to be under the influence in order to be bold enough to try to take the crown of sovereignty that belongs to God alone, but Ephraim's priests and prophets were haughty enough to think that they could cheat punishment and death (Isaiah 28:15). No wonder Isaiah referred to them as drunkards — they were

22

inebriated with self-deception and blindness to God's coming wrath, and they corrupted the rest of the people. Arrogance stops up the ears, making good counsel sound like babbling (Isaiah 28:11–13). We've seen this before—when the hubris of famous business moguls, actors, or athletes have blinded them to their own mortality, leading them to disastrous consequences. In order to reflect on matters of life and death, one needs a sober mind and a contrite heart. In contrast to dozing drunkards, clueless about God's movement in the world, Christians must live Spirit-filled lives (Ephesians 5:18) with a sober discernment of the world and God's righteous judgment (1 Thessalonians 5:2–8).

Isaiah 29

Woe, O Ariel, Ariel the city where David once camped!
Add year to year, observe your feasts on schedule. —*Isaiah 29:1*

The prophecy of Isaiah 29 is addressed to "Ariel"—Isaiah's poetic description of Jerusalem. *Ariel* can be translated to mean "altar hearth," the central point of sacrifices in the temple of God. Jerusalem was supposed to be the geographical center of worship for the people of Judah, but God could find no true worshipers there. Empty ritual replaced the awe, dedication, and surrender of the people to God, and lip service snuffed out sincere prayer and praise (Isaiah 29:13–14). The "altar hearth" of Jerusalem grew cold. Hundreds of years later, when Jesus talked with a Samaritan woman about worship, she also emphasized geography (John 4:19–20). Jesus focused on true worship trumping ritual: "But an hour is coming, and now is, when the true worshipers will worship the Father in spirit and truth; for such people the Father seeks to be His worshipers" (4:23). God is not impressed with our buildings; He's not wowed by our religiosity. Without

love for Him, rituals and edifices are just clanging brass . . .
hollow (1 Corinthians 13:1–3).

Isaiah 30

For thus the Lord GOD, the Holy One of Israel, has said,
"In repentance and rest you will be saved,
In quietness and trust is your strength."
But you were not willing. —Isaiah 30:15

We live in a DIY—Do It Yourself—culture with how-to vid-
eos and virtual drawing boards, armchair experts and big-box
home improvement chains. We want to find solutions and execute them, and perhaps we've experienced a measure of success
that way. The people of Israel were seduced by the same DIY
mentality, to their peril. Instead of trusting that the God who
led them out of Egypt could protect them from their adversaries, they decided to *return to Egypt* by asking them for security
and resources rather than calling on the Lord. They spun their
wheels, fretting and plotting, while God invited them to repent
of their sin of straying from God, and to instead rest in Him with
quiet faith. Doesn't it sound a lot more appealing to rest quietly
in the Lord? There is peace in surrendering to the truth that we
cannot do it all ourselves.

Isaiah 31

Woe to those who go down to Egypt for help
And rely on horses,
And trust in chariots because they are many
And in horsemen because they are very strong,
But they do not look to the Holy One of Israel, nor seek the LORD!
—Isaiah 31:1

In Isaiah 31, the prophecy continued to highlight the contrast between trusting in God and trusting in Egypt, idols, chariots, or horses—in anything other than Him. God emphasized that the Assyrians, Israel's looming threat, would be defeated, but by God rather than through a hasty, faithless treaty between Israel and Egypt. One can imagine how difficult it would have been for the Israelites to rely solely on God when faced with a fierce foe. The natural instinct is either fight or flight, but God gave them a third choice—faith. Faith is sometimes like taking a step into the invisible and trusting God for the results. God had demonstrated to Israel His loyal love and deliverance several times through military victory, yet they chose not to trust Him. How many times have we ignored the prompting to trust God when challenges have loomed large? How many times before has God proven faithful? *Trust Him.*

Isaiah 32

For a fool speaks nonsense,
And his heart inclines toward wickedness:
To practice ungodliness and to speak error against the LORD,
To keep the hungry person unsatisfied
And to withhold drink from the thirsty. —Isaiah 32:6

How would you define the term *fool*? Would you define it as a lack of wisdom or discretion? Is a fool someone without knowledge? How does God define the fool? In Isaiah 32, Isaiah contrasted the princes of justice and righteousness and the Provider of security, God, with the fool and the rogue. The fool, in God's estimation, is not one who merely lacks knowledge but is a windbag who withholds from the needy those things needed for sustenance. The rogue is wicked because he slanders the poor whom he ought to be helping (Isaiah 32:7). In God's economy, the poor and needy don't earn His scorn but rather those who lead with corruption and selfishness do. Wise believers are about our Father's business: feeding the hungry, clothing the naked, and advocating for the voiceless as compassionate acts of worship.

Isaiah 33

Your heart will meditate on terror:
"Where is he who counts?
Where is he who weighs?
Where is he who counts the towers?" —Isaiah 33:18

The Assyrian conquest was wicked, and Isaiah 33 expresses God's warning that the atrocities committed by Assyria would not go unanswered—that God would vindicate Zion. But the conquest would leave scars on the psyche of the people whose lingering fears would be marked by post-traumatic stress. Assyrian officials counted and weighed, tallying Israelite goods to assess how much to tax them for their king's tribute. While the people of Zion would live in fear of foreign powers for a while, Isaiah prophesied that God would bring restoration. Now, they were a boat swept away by wind (Isaiah 33:23), but in the future, they would be an established dwelling, an unmovable tent (33:20). God disciplines us because He loves us and because He wants to train us for righteousness, not because He enjoys seeing His people suffer (Hebrews 12:11). His intention for us is peace, not trauma.

Isaiah 34

For the LORD has a day of vengeance,
A year of recompense for the cause of Zion. — *Isaiah 34:8*

Edom, one of the first enemies of Israel, symbolized all of the nations opposed to God. The violent imagery of bloody sacrifices exacted by the sword of God is an overwhelming reminder of His holy wrath and justice. God *will* avenge His people; He won't stand by and let the enemy triumph. The prophecy is gruesome — God's sword drips with blood and the fat of those slaughtered. How do we reconcile this wrathful God with the God of love? It is hard for us to hear the harmony of God's wrath and justice, His mercy and love. Beyond this difficulty is the truth that God's ways are just and good, and His enemies are our enemies. He searches hearts and can differentiate between a Judas and a Peter. Though both disciples sinned bitterly against Jesus, only Peter repented. Though condemnation and a thirst for revenge are natural reactions to evil, we can shed our desire for vengeance, knowing that God is the perfect Judge.

Isaiah 35

Then the eyes of the blind will be opened
And the ears of the deaf will be unstopped.
Then the lame will leap like a deer,
And the tongue of the mute will shout for joy.
For waters will break forth in the wilderness
And streams in the Arabah. — *Isaiah 35:5–6*

We have all likely attended a sporting event, where we cheered on our favorite team when they were down and needed to score . . . and especially when they made the winning touchdown, goal, or home run and the crowd went wild. This chapter is *more* jubilant and life-giving than any game. God knew that the Israelites would need a dose of good news after hearing the dim oracle over Edom, so He described the miraculous splendor that awaits the redeemed of the Lord—the good news that devastation and desert will be transformed into lushness! God's people felt exploited and made small by their enemies, threatened and defenseless. But it's not over—they will joyfully shout (Isaiah 35:10)! Isaiah told the afflicted to comfort each other with this truth (35:4). Similarly, the apostle Paul told believers to "comfort one another" with that very fact—*it's not over yet.* Jesus is coming again, and we will be with Him forever (1 Thessalonians 4:16–18). Let's remember the promises of God during our dark times and encourage our fellow believers—and ourselves—that God always keeps His word.

Isaiah 36

"Thus says the king, 'Do not let Hezekiah deceive you, for he will not be able to deliver you; nor let Hezekiah make you trust in the LORD, saying, "The LORD will surely deliver us, this city will not be given into the hand of the king of Assyria."'"   *—Isaiah 36:14–15*

Isaiah 36 describes Assyria's haughty opposition to the people of God. Repeatedly, Assyria's representative, Rabshakeh, decreed, "Thus says the king of Assyria," as a preamble to his demands for Judah's surrender (Isaiah 36:4, 13, 16). When Judah's representatives encouraged Rabshakeh to speak Aramaic, he opted instead to shout in Hebrew of Judah's doom (36:13). He intended to mortify everyone within the sound of his voice with tales of other gods and of nations defeated by Assyria. He attempted to separate Judah's inhabitants from their God and their king. But Rabshakeh's plainly-spoken words inadvertently worked in God's favor, because everyone in Judah would know it was the Lord's intercession that caused Assyria not to attack, 185,000 of Assyria's troops to die, and Assyria's king to be murdered (Isaiah 37:36–38). Powerful and godless people can try to intimidate believers with their bravado. Don't listen! Instead, take your cares to God (Philippians 4:6–7), and give Him room to fight your battles.

Isaiah 37

"Therefore, thus says the LORD concerning the king of Assyria, 'He will not come to this city or shoot an arrow there; and he will not come before it with a shield, or throw up a siege ramp against it. By the way that he came, by the same he will return, and he will not come to this city,' declares the LORD." — Isaiah 37:33–34

The drama of chapter 36 spilled into chapter 37, where Judah's representatives tell King Hezekiah about Assyria's threats. What would King Hezekiah do? Would he believe King Sennacherib or Yahweh for security? Hezekiah was a good king, and he prayed for God to intervene against those who would blaspheme His holy name (Isaiah 37:17, 20). When Hezekiah received a troubling word, his first response was to go to the house of God. God's gracious response was immediate and precise — not only did Sennacherib not lay siege to the city (37:37), but God struck dead 185,000 of Sennacherib's troops (37:36), and Sennacherib was killed by his own sons (37:38). God honored the prayer of His servant, Hezekiah, and He defended His covenant with David (37:35). Our circumstances are nowhere near Hezekiah's, but we can learn well from his example: when trouble arises, where do we head first? Let's pursue God in prayer as our first response.

Isaiah 38

"Go and say to Hezekiah, 'Thus says the LORD, the God of your father David, "I have heard your prayer, I have seen your tears; behold, I will add fifteen years to your life. I will deliver you and this city from the hand of the king of Assyria; and I will defend this city."'"
—Isaiah 38:5–6

King Hezekiah's story is a case study in how the Lord desired to treat His people. In preceding chapters, Isaiah's prophecies railed against the unjust and profane but commended those who took up for the poor, who sought justice, who revered God's name in both word and deed. Hezekiah was a man who trusted God in the face of Assyrian threat, and God honored that trust. But as Hezekiah lay dying, Isaiah told him under God's authority to get his affairs in order. Hezekiah's tearful response—the prayer of the righteous—moved God to give him fifteen additional years of life and an added guarantee of Jerusalem's safety. The object lesson is *not* that God will increase our years whenever we ask Him, but that the Lord's ear is inclined to His children, and our emotions and circumstances will never be neglected by our loving Father. As with Hezekiah, God's favor toward His children ought to move us to praise God.

Isaiah 39

Then Hezekiah said to Isaiah, "The word of the LORD which you have spoken is good." For he thought, "For there will be peace and truth in my days."
—Isaiah 39:8

There is *major* foreshadowing happening in Isaiah 39: a fully recovered King Hezekiah received a well-wisher, a prince of Babylon, to whom Hezekiah showed all of his palatial estate and possessions (Isaiah 39:2). The prophet Isaiah, alarmed, warned Hezekiah that Babylon will come in and carry away all that he had shown off that day (39:6–7), but Hezekiah wasn't worried because he'd be dead by the time the prophecy came true. Hezekiah—a good king—had nevertheless become so caught up in his present that he neglected to plan for the future of the kingdom. Hezekiah fasted when confronted with Assyria, but he didn't respond with prayer and fasting when confronted with the future turmoil with Babylon. Though he was a good king, Hezekiah proved himself not to be the Branch of whom Isaiah prophesied (11:1). Even devout leaders can fail in spiritual matters. Believers shoudn't put their leaders on a pedestal—they will surely fall off. Instead, we can pray for their wisdom and obedience to God.

Isaiah 40

Why do you say, O Jacob, and assert, O Israel,
"My way is hidden from the LORD,
And the justice due me escapes the notice of my God"?
Do you not know? Have you not heard?
The Everlasting God, the LORD, the Creator of the ends of the earth
Does not become weary or tired.
His understanding is inscrutable.
He gives strength to the weary,
And to him who lacks might He increases power. —Isaiah 40:27–29

Isaiah 40 begins a new series of pronouncements—of hope, restoration, and revelations of the Servant of God. This chapter is among the most beautiful encouragements to the people of Jerusalem ever written. Where should their hope lie? In the inscrutable and all-powerful Lord God. He defies definition and needs no counsel. As God's power and knowledge is abundant and eternal, His commitment to love and restore is just as abounding. If we ever feel like our troubles remain unnoticed by God, we must remember Isaiah's proclamation that God's thinking resembles *nothing* of this world—He is completely other. How much of our frustration with God is a result of our not comprehending who He is? The wisest person on earth cannot love, keep promises, deliver, or counsel like the Lord. This is why Isaiah wrote in verse 8, "The grass withers, the flower fades, but the word of our God stands forever."

Isaiah 41

"Do not fear, you worm Jacob, you men of Israel;
I will help you," declares the Lord, "and your Redeemer is the Holy
*   One of Israel.*
Behold, I have made you a new, sharp threshing sledge with double
*   edges;*
You will thresh the mountains and pulverize them,
And will make the hills like chaff."   —Isaiah 41:14–15

Picture a lowly worm, wriggling its soft body through supple dirt, leaving behind the tiniest of holes. That worm won't make much of an impact on the earth. God compared Israel to a worm and promised to transform the nation into a threshing sledge that would pulverize and winnow mountains. A threshing sledge was used to glean wheat kernels from their husks. Wheat kernels are nestled firmly in a plant "fortress," so extracting them requires weight, sharpness, and force (the opposite of a worm!). In Isaiah's time, a donkey pulled this flat, rock-pocked plank over wheat, tearing into the plant and displacing the kernels. Can you imagine the strength of a sledge compared to a worm? Only the transforming power of a redeeming God can cause a worm to thresh mountains. Yes, we're weak, vulnerable, small — but we have the power to faithfully glorify God in our relationships, finances, charity, and child-rearing. Our God, who commands and judges the "coastlands" (Isaiah 41:1), is the force, weight, and sharpness empowering us for His glory.

Isaiah 42

"Behold, My Servant, whom I uphold;
My chosen one in whom My soul delights.
I have put My Spirit upon Him;
He will bring forth justice to the nations."   *—Isaiah 42:1*

Isaiah introduces the theme of God's Servant in chapter 42. Where in the previous chapter God described His sovereignty over the idol-worshiping coastlands — considered to be the geographical "ends of the earth" and the domain of the Gentiles — in this chapter, Isaiah describes the Servant as the one who will humbly and gently bring justice to the nations (Isaiah 42:2–3). God also referred to Israel as His "servant" (42:19), but where Israel had failed to glorify God in its witness to the nations, this forthcoming Servant would succeed. Because we live on this side of His first coming, we know that Jesus is God's Servant of Isaiah 42:1, who meekly submitted to being put to death on a cross, executing justice for the nations by bearing their punishment Himself. In His mercy, God still chose to use His covenant people to open the eyes and ears of those deceived by idolatry (42:6–7) through Jesus the Messiah. In the same way, God chooses to use us as witnesses for Christ to our neighbors and to the nations (Matthew 28:19–20; Acts 1:8).

Isaiah 43

"Do not fear, for I am with you;
I will bring your offspring from the east,
And gather you from the west.
I will say to the north, 'Give them up!'
And to the south, 'Do not hold them back.'
Bring My sons from afar
And My daughters from the ends of the earth,
Everyone who is called by My name,
And whom I have created for My glory,
Whom I have formed, even whom I have made." —Isaiah 43:5–7

The circumstances the children of Israel faced—warfare, exile, shame—understandably caused them to fear for their future. Would they ever come out from under the consequences of betraying God? The sweet words of redemption from Isaiah 43 must have soothed their ears when God said, "I am with you." God promised to gather His people together again; their sin was not a perpetual death sentence. Can we comprehend the life-giving power of God calling us by name? He calls us out of spiritual death to life (Ephesians 2:4–6). He calls us out of a spiritual holding pattern and into a destiny of useful, godly service, as He did with Moses (Exodus 3:4). He calls us to second chances after failure, as He did with Peter (John 21:15–17). He called Lazarus

Isaiah 48

"Behold, I have refined you, but not as silver;
I have tested you in the furnace of affliction.
"For My own sake, for My own sake, I will act;
For how can My name be profaned?
And My glory I will not give to another."   —*Isaiah 48:10–11*

Verses 4, 5, and 10 of Isaiah 48 place a special emphasis on metal. Bronze and iron were the most common metals of the day, forged to make weapons, fishing anchors, and bowls. Idols were sometimes made of bronze, so in His description of Israel in verses 4 and 5, God may have been drawing attention to the nation's idol-worshiping past in addition to its stubbornness. In verse 10, God referred to Himself as a refiner. Other prophecies (Zechariah 13:9; Malachi 3:3) describe how God's refining would produce righteous worshipers. In this passage, however, God is clear that He will *not* refine the people of Israel as silver, because in that obstinate generation, no silver was found, just dross. Rather, He placed them in the furnace of affliction. Malachi 3:6 reads, "For I, the LORD, do not change; therefore you, O sons of Jacob, are not *consumed*" (emphasis added). God afflicted them, and yet restrained His wrath (Isaiah 48:9) for the sake of His Name. The dross of sin that saturates the lives of humankind would have caused us all to perish, but for God's mercy! When we feel helpless, even when we go through trials, we can still worship the Lord, thankful that His hand of protection is still upon us.

Isaiah 49

He says, "It is too small a thing that You should be My Servant
To raise up the tribes of Jacob and to restore the preserved ones of
*   Israel;*
I will also make You a light of the nations
So that My salvation may reach to the end of the earth."

—Isaiah 49:6

How magnificent is this Servant whom Isaiah detailed in
Isaiah 49! Through Him, salvation is available to everyone on
earth. This Redeemer will restore Israel to its land (Isaiah 49:8)
and shepherd the nation, giving its people rest, food, and water
(49:10). Hope and restoration burst forth from the chapter.
At a time when Israel could be best described as the "barren,
exile, wanderer" (49:21), the Lord promised esteem, return, and
rest. Zion—representing the people of Israel—felt abandoned
(49:14). But the people of Israel were not forgotten; *better* than a
mother tenderly caring for her newborn baby was the Lord God
to His people (49:15). We must take a moment to absorb the
measure of God's love for us. He sent His Servant as a light for
us, the nations. God's tender care includes salvation, not only
for Israel but for us. For *us*.

Isaiah 50

The Lord GOD has given Me the tongue of disciples,
That I may know how to sustain the weary one with a word.
He awakens Me morning by morning,
He awakens My ear to listen as a disciple.
The Lord GOD has opened My ear;
And I was not disobedient
Nor did I turn back.   *—Isaiah 50:4–5*

We have all been in the depths of sadness, loneliness, or despair, only to hear an encouraging word just at the right time — insightful conversation that helped us feel hope again. Healing words hold power. God's Servant brings that kind of life-giving hope to God's people. Because He is constantly obedient, that hope is dogged and unrelenting. It's the kind of hope that illumines the darkness. The hope the Servant gives is not dependent on the approval of humankind (Isaiah 50:6); it's based on the Lord's directives and is empowered by Him. What is this hope? The Lord has absolute power — and willingness — to deliver (50:2). While Jesus was scourged and hung upon the cross, He *had* to depend on His Father for life-giving vindication. The Servant, Jesus, is the preeminent example of hope that does not disappoint (Romans 5:5). Look around: are there weary ones around us who could use an encouraging word? Let's lift their chins with words of hope. Do you need encouragement? You'll find it in the Scriptures.

Isaiah 51

Thus says your Lord, the Lord, even your God
Who contends for His people,
"Behold, I have taken out of your hand the cup of reeling,
The chalice of My anger;
You will never drink it again."   *— Isaiah 51:22*

Isaiah described the Israelites as exiled, powerless, and fearful. Still cringing in fear of foreign invaders and God, who was no longer protecting them, they drank deep from the chalice of God's anger (Isaiah 51:17). God came near, but this time, He came to replace that chalice with His comfort (51:22). For the ransomed, God's salvation will never end (51:6–8)! The ransomed — those

41

for whom God has paid to set free—never again need to fear humanity (Isaiah 51:12–13). We must ask ourselves: Do we live in fear of God, or is He our comfort? In Jesus, we are ransomed, set free. His yoke is easy, His burden light (Matthew 11:30). In Him, we are also sealed by the Holy Spirit, our Comforter (John 14:16 KJV). Jesus drank the cup of wrath (Matthew 26:39) so that He could offer His followers the cup of the New Covenant.

Isaiah 52

Just as many were astonished at you, My people,
So His appearance was marred more than any man
And His form more than the sons of men. —Isaiah 52:14

The kingdom of God is astonishing to humankind—it's unexpected and generous and humble. The Servant would astonish kings, even with His marred appearance. No doubt, the foreign nations' thoughts about the one, true God were tied to how they viewed Israel. How could an all-powerful God bring His beloved nation to such humble circumstances if He's real? We question God, millennia later: How could a good God send His Son to die? In the kingdom of God, those who wish to save their lives, lose them; the first are last. The kingdom of God is powerful because its subjects are not self-seeking spectacles—they make God the focal point and honor Him by honoring others. The Servant would be exalted because of how He served others, even to the point of death—an astounding action for a king. Do we astonish others by the way we reflect Jesus in our daily lives?

Isaiah 53

As a result of the anguish of His soul,
He will see it and be satisfied;
By His knowledge the Righteous One,
My Servant, will justify the many,
As He will bear their iniquities.   —Isaiah 53:11

One of the most widely read passages of Scripture, Isaiah 53, is a description of the Suffering Servant. Isaiah continued the previous chapter's theme of the people's astonishment that the Servant was homely to look upon (Isaiah 53:2). Instead of associating with opulence, He was acquainted with sorrow, grief, and oppression (53:3, 7). Isaiah 53:1 describes Messiah, the shoot (of Jesse, like in 11:1). When Isaiah beautifully described God's Servant-Messiah in this gospel-tinged prophecy, he had no name, no Person to attach to it. We do! The people of Israel were astounded at Jesus' claim to be Messiah, in part because He showed up as a lamb instead of a lion. He didn't topple the political oppressor. He gave no deferential treatment to Pharisees but justified sinners who were desperate to be set free. He wore a thorny crown, and His robes were flayed skin and royal, red blood. What great love at such great cost! "But God demonstrates His own love toward us, in that while we were yet sinners, Christ died for us" (Romans 5:8).

Isaiah 54

"No weapon that is formed against you will prosper;
And every tongue that accuses you in judgment you will condemn.
This is the heritage of the servants of the Lord,
And their vindication is from Me," declares the Lord. —Isaiah 54:17

King David declared in Psalm 103:2, "Bless the LORD, O my soul, and forget none of His benefits." Isaiah 54 is a shout for joy to the Lord, remembering all His benefits. In the ancient Near East, the barren woman was considered cursed and broken. Children were a sign of prosperity and were insurance that the parents would be taken care of in their old age. Israel without God was like a barren widow (Isaiah 54:1). Oh, but *with* God, they had an unparalleled heritage: one of vindication, prosperity; one where the terror of living without God would be a bygone memory, never to be repeated (54:9–10). In the millennium, Israel will receive the heritage of God's active presence. Christians have received an inheritance of blessings (Colossians 1:12–13). The Holy Spirit indwells us and guarantees God's ever-presence in our lives (Ephesians 1:13–14). We are not alone. We are loved. God *never* opposes His own. And the best is yet to come. Don't forget His benefits!

Isaiah 55

Let the wicked forsake his way
And the unrighteous man his thoughts;
And let him return to the LORD,
And He will have compassion on him,
And to our God,
For He will abundantly pardon.   —*Isaiah 55:7*

Haven't we heard people attempt to distinguish the God of the Old Testament from the God of the New Testament? The Old Testament God, they say, is vengeful, angry, and merciless; while the New Testament God is full of love, compassion, and forgiveness. One of the reasons it's vital to read the whole Bible is to know the truth about God—He is consistent. In Isaiah 55, God called out to His children to give them good food (Isaiah 55:2). God is a loving Father, urging His children to choose wisely, because He would much rather lavish us with good things than punish us. In the New Testament, Jesus expressed the same sentiment (Luke 13:34). Too often, God's children are tone-deaf to His messages and oblivious to His patience. We ignore the Bible the way the Israelites ignored the prophets, seeking more "modern" methods to govern our lives. To ignore God's Word leaves us unsatisfied.

Isaiah 56

*"Also the foreigners who join themselves to the L*ORD*,*
To minister to Him, and to love the name of the Lord,
To be His servants, every one who keeps from profaning the sabbath
And holds fast My covenant;
Even those I will bring to My holy mountain
And make them joyful in My house of prayer.
Their burnt offerings and their sacrifices will be acceptable on My
    altar;
For My house will be called a house of prayer for all the peoples."
—Isaiah 56:6–7

Isaiah 56:6–7 is worth shouting about! After reading chapter after chapter about God's beautiful promises to bless Israel, an outsider might wonder, *Is there hope for me?* (Isaiah 56:3). God's answer is a resounding yes! His house will be a house of prayer for *all* people. (Perhaps Philip shared this passage with the Ethiopian eunuch after explaining Isaiah 53 in Acts 8:27–39!) This passage is for those like the Canaanite woman in Matthew 15:22–28 who, because of her faith, was willing to risk embarrassment and argue with Jesus that her daughter might be made well—accepting the designation of a dog just to get some crumbs. What humility! And such a humble mind-set is a defining characteristic of the kingdom of God. This passage is for *us!* God's offer of salvation is one way that He keeps His promise that He will bless the nations through Abraham (Genesis 12:3). We are not dogs but co-heirs: "If you belong to Christ, then you are Abraham's descendants, heirs according to promise" (Galatians 3:29)! Praise God for including us in His plan.

Isaiah 57

For thus says the high and exalted One
Who lives forever, whose name is Holy,
"I dwell on a high and holy place,
And also with the contrite and lowly of spirit
In order to revive the spirit of the lowly
And to revive the heart of the contrite."   *—Isaiah 57:15*

In chapter 56, God reassures the righteous, but in chapter 57, He warns the wicked. God overturns the values of the godless and renders the world's ways as idolatrous folly (Romans 1:22–23). The wicked cannot distinguish good people from bad and are too haughty to recognize the danger of ridiculing the righteous (Isaiah 57:4). The wicked dedicate all their energy to self-indulgence and idolatry (57:10). Do we recognize in our own world what Isaiah's prophecy warned against: self-indulgence, sexual immorality, vanity? It's rampant in our culture. God cuts right through the shallow quests for pleasure to pursue our souls, to commune with the contrite, to make His place with the lowly. So should we. Believers ought to steer clear of pride and the clamor for stuff and power, and instead pursue that which God values—kindness, justice, love, and devotion to Him.

Isaiah 58

"Is this not the fast which I choose,
To loosen the bonds of wickedness,
To undo the bands of the yoke,
And to let the oppressed go free
And break every yoke?"   *—Isaiah 58:6*

Second Corinthians 3:17 reads, "Where the Spirit of the Lord is, there is liberty." The people of Israel were bound by religious chains—engaging in fasting for the purpose of impressing others rather than honoring God. God's intention for fasting is that people are freed from the chains of empty ritualism through our giving and receiving, through our considering others first by meeting their needs. Godly fasting includes self-sacrificing care, compassion, and love for others. The people's motivating question in fasting was, "Who may I surpass in my religiosity?" while godly motivation prompts people to ask, "To whom may I be a neighbor?" God desires for His people to be beacons of selfless righteousness—as portrayed in Jesus' parable about the good Samaritan (Luke 10:25–37). God gives us the prescription for a satisfied soul in Isaiah 58: to worship Him with our hearts and to genuinely care for others. If we do these things, we are *always* guaranteed to be in God's will and receive His blessing.

Isaiah 59

Yes, truth is lacking;
And he who turns aside from evil makes himself a prey.
Now the LORD saw,
And it was displeasing in His sight that there was no justice.
And He saw that there was no man,
And was astonished that there was no one to intercede;
Then His own arm brought salvation to Him,
And His righteousness upheld Him.   — *Isaiah 59:15–16*

Israel needed a redeemer and a warrior, because injustice overwhelmed the land and created a gulf between its people and God (Isaiah 59:2). This chapter of Isaiah depicts the confession of Israel; the nation's failure to protect truth, its miscarriages of justice, and its penchant for lying. The previous chapter dealt with Israel's deficiency in worship; this chapter highlights how far Israel had strayed from caring for its neighbors. Even God's own representative, Isaiah, couldn't bear the responsibility of turning God's people back to Him. When God could find no one to stand for justice, He girded up *Himself* to be Israel's Redeemer and Warrior. We on this side of Jesus' resurrection may read these words casually, but Isaiah's audience had long forgotten that God had been their Redeemer in Egypt, and during their years in the wilderness, and during their crossing over into the Promised Land. We are also prone to forget that Jesus redeemed us and is coming again to war with and conquer evil. Do we live in light of His coming? Do we live in constant gratitude for His redemption?

Isaiah 60

"Violence will not be heard again in your land,
Nor devastation or destruction within your borders;
But you will call your walls salvation, and your gates praise."

—Isaiah 60:18

When one reflects on the history and present circumstances of Israel, what likely comes to mind? Conflict? Religious epicenter? Border disputes? A place of worship? Violence? Even modern-day Israel's borders seem continually contentious. The state of affairs in Isaiah's day were hostile for different reasons, but one aspect was similar: peace in Judah seemed unattainable, an impossible dream. In the future millennium, the world will finally see Israel function fully as God intended, and it will be known as a place of peace. Just as Israel will be fully realized to glorify God, in the future, believers will no longer have to struggle with their sin nature and will wholly glorify God. When people think of Christians, what crosses their minds? Whatever the answer, we should remember that we are God's work in progress. When He begins a work, He is faithful to perfect it (Philippians 1:6)! When He is done, believers in Jesus will be spotless (Ephesians 5:27).

Isaiah 61

For as the earth brings forth its sprouts,
And as a garden causes the things sown in it to spring up,
So the Lord GOD will cause righteousness and praise
To spring up before all the nations.

—Isaiah 61:11

When Jesus declared to the teachers in the temple His public ministry, He opened the scroll and began to read this chapter of Isaiah (Luke 4:18–21). How poetic! Jesus was the root that Isaiah spoke of in chapters 11 and 53. In chapter 61, Isaiah prophesied of righteousness and praise "springing up" just as a plant would. This chapter revels in God's deliverance. Notice that in Luke 4, Jesus closed the scroll before reading about the "vengeance of our God" (Isaiah 61:2). The time between Jesus' opening the scroll in the temple and the time to come is the pause between prophecy and fulfillment in Isaiah 61:2. We live in a time when, at any moment, the rapture could occur after which then the advent of Christ's second coming and the vengeance of our God can begin to unfold. We wait expectantly for Jesus to fulfill everything Isaiah promised, knowing that God cannot help but cultivate and grow righteousness in His creation.

Isaiah 62

It will no longer be said to you, "Forsaken,"
Nor to your land will it any longer be said, "Desolate";
But you will be called, "My delight is in her,"
And your land, "Married";
For the LORD delights in you,
And to Him your land will be married.   *— Isaiah 62:4*

We crave tales where love triumphs over conflict, where the gentle pursuit of a trustworthy man melts the heart of a woman with a checkered past, transforming her. The people of Israel were religiously promiscuous (Ezekiel 23:37) and humbled by displacement from their land. God promised not to leave Israel humiliated. In His love, God committed to take back Israel and, like a bride, wash her, heal her wounds, and dress her in radiant white. The marriage metaphor used in this chapter — though not meant to be conceived of as sexual in any way — is the closest concept we have to the mystery of God's love for the redeemed.

This metaphor is also highlighted in Christ's love for the church (Ephesians 5:32). When we understand the depth of selfless love with which the Lord lavishes us, we cannot help but glow in gratitude. The marriage supper of the Lamb—a divine reception to end all receptions—is coming! We can clothe ourselves in righteous deeds to make ourselves ready for the Groom who delights in us (Revelation 19:7–8).

Isaiah 63

"I trod down the peoples in My anger
And made them drunk in My wrath,
And I poured out their lifeblood on the earth."
I shall make mention of the lovingkindnesses of the LORD, the praises
*   of the LORD,*
According to all that the LORD has granted us,
And the great goodness toward the house of Israel,
Which He has granted them according to His compassion
And according to the abundance of His lovingkindnesses.

—Isaiah 63:6–7

What a gulf that seems to exist between verses 6 and 7! Verse 6 is the culmination of God's wrath upon the godless—He will trample them like grapes; while verse 7 extols the compassion and loving-kindness of God. Why fatal justice for one group and tender mercy for the other? If all are sinners, why does God confer preferential treatment on some? The answer lies in Isaiah's prayer at the end of chapter 63, where he acknowledged the loving, protective character of God (Isaiah 63:7, 8, 16), admitted the sins of his people (63:10), and asked the Lord to be the God who loves and delivers just as He did in the exodus (63:11–14, 17). All people sin, but those who repent are justified by God. The

Lord delights in those who come to Him with a contrite heart (57:15), confessing their sin (1 John 1:9), and acknowledging His hand in their past, present, and future (Proverbs 3:5–6).

Isaiah 64

Will You restrain Yourself at these things, O Lord?
Will You keep silent and afflict us beyond measure?   —Isaiah 64:12

Who are we to ask God questions? After all, we are finite—dust. It's especially intriguing that the prophet who relayed so many messages about the indisputable sovereignty of God (Isaiah 45:9–10) would so boldly end this passage with a question: *Are You really going to let this keep happening, Lord?* Yet, the Lord was not displeased with Isaiah for asking. Why? God looks at the heart (2 Samuel 16:7)—the motivation and posture behind questions. Isaiah sought to see the rescue of his people in part to protect the name of God. He was aware of Israel's unworthiness (Isaiah 64:6) but begged for mercy the way God's servant Moses had advocated for Israel (Exodus 32:11–14). God wants us to communicate honestly with Him. Isaiah teaches us to pause and, before firing off questions, ask ourselves, "What's my motivation?" Are we seeking God's glory or merely our comfort?

Isaiah 65

"I have spread out My hands all day long to a rebellious people,
Who walk in the way which is not good, following their own
    thoughts."   —Isaiah 65:2

Proverbs 14:12 says, "There is a way which seems right to a man, but its end is the way of death." Why do we usually find an abundance of flowers at a funeral, flanking the casket of the deceased?

These flowers attempt to gently mask an ugly truth. Death is *not* good. From before the fall, God created humanity to commune with Him eternally. Isaiah 65 draws a dichotomy between the servants of God and those who are accursed. The accursed are those who, even in the face of God's constant pursuit (Isaiah 65:1–5), choose to live separated from Him, opting instead to do what's right in their own eyes. They are essentially the walking dead. God's servants, in contrast, choose life by walking humbly with their God (Micah 6:8). Jesus indicted the Pharisees for being "whitewashed tombs" because, like their forefathers, their hearts were far from God as they reveled in their self-righteousness. As the redeemed of God, we are *graced* with a relationship with God (Ephesians 2:8–9)—*He* is the sustainer of our abundant lives (1 Timothy 1:14–15). With this reminder, we should live each day in dependence, joy, and intimacy with our gracious God.

Isaiah 66

"Then they will go forth and look
On the corpses of the men
Who have transgressed against Me.
For their worm will not die
And their fire will not be quenched;
And they will be an abhorrence to all mankind." —Isaiah 66:24

The book of Isaiah ends on a somber note—a reader can almost smell the stench of burning flesh and picture the wriggling gyrations of insatiable maggots feeding on the corpses of the condemned. The redeemed will be able to view the fate of those who are lost. What an unimaginable, hopeless scene! The prophet Isaiah makes the message of God clear: trust God for life; ignore Him to your peril. The eternal future of each person is contingent on how he or she responds to the Lord. Those who put their trust in God will be comforted by Him as a mother comforts her child (Isaiah 66:13). To honor our compassionate God, we can be enthusiastic in encouraging believers to seek God first and in sharing the gospel with those who don't know Jesus. God asks, "Whom shall I send, and who will go for Us?" (6:8). May our answer be, "Here we are, Lord. Send us!"

Jeremiah

Jeremiah 1

"Before I formed you in the womb I knew you,
And before you were born I consecrated you;
I have appointed you a prophet to the nations." —*Jeremiah 1:5*

Jeremiah had a destiny. God called Jeremiah to remind Israel of its divine purpose to be a light to the nations. But this call didn't fall on Jeremiah because he was in the right place at the right time or because he was the only faithful one left in Judah. The Lord formed Jeremiah in his mother's womb for His purpose, lining up Jeremiah's DNA and knitting together his personality and his gifts. God created the prophet to the nations with a sensitive heart and firm conviction so that Jeremiah would fulfill his mission to proclaim God's message. Yes, Jeremiah had a destiny—and so do we. Though God hasn't called us as prophets, and most Christians live simple, anonymous lives, God stitched together our personalities, passions, and abilities for His purpose. Let's reflect on God's specific calling on our lives and begin to fulfill it with the sensitivity and conviction of Jeremiah.

Jeremiah 2

"Your own wickedness will correct you,
And your apostasies will reprove you;
Know therefore and see that it is evil and bitter
For you to forsake the LORD your God,
And the dread of Me is not in you," declares the Lord GOD of hosts.
—*Jeremiah 2:19*

We reap what we sow. The history of God's people proves this maxim true. Though God had extended mercy for hundreds of years while His people rejected Him, the time had come for judgment. For Israel's violation of the Mosaic Covenant, God's people had to face the promised curses (Deuteronomy 28:47–48). God sent Israel into captivity so they would remember His love, justice, and mercy. No one can escape the results of his or her actions. Even for Christians, God doesn't wipe away the consequences of our decisions. Like the heartburn that follows an enormous meal, the consequences of sin are indeed painful. Though the Lord forgives all our sins, our sins set in motion chain reactions that affect not only us but also countless others around us. For example, that lie we once told can come back to haunt us. These repercussions from our sins serve as forms of discipline to reprove and correct us.

Jeremiah 3

" 'Return, O faithless sons,' declares the LORD;
'For I am a master to you,
And I will take you one from a city and two from a family,
And I will bring you to Zion.' " —*Jeremiah 3:14*

God's people were at one time numerous and followed Him faithfully. But by Jeremiah's time, the majority followed wood and stone idols. Though the inhabitants of Judah had violated the covenant and wandered far from Him, God promised to one day extend grace to His covenant people. But only a small remnant, representing God's faithful, refined people, would return. Motivated by love for his people and faith in God's coming judgment and redemption, Jeremiah shared God's message, and it almost cost him his life. Centuries later, Jesus reminded us that there are two roads to eternity: a wide, six-lane highway headed toward destruction and a narrow, country road destined for life (Matthew 7:13–14). We need to call out to those on the highway—sacrificing our comfort, pride, and agenda—to help travelers find the narrow road that leads to life. We need to love the people God has placed in our lives enough to tell them where those two roads lead.

Jeremiah 4

I looked on the earth, and behold, it was formless and void;
And to the heavens, and they had no light. —Jeremiah 4:23

The land that God had created to satisfy and bless His people had been polluted with false worship. The light that the Lord had shone the first morning of creation had been snuffed out by Judah's injustice. God had no choice but to start over—to kick His people out of their land and to release His wrath. The mountains He had formed to reveal His grandeur shook at the sound of His anger. And the people He loved perished before their enemies. Sin inevitably leads to chaos, disorder, and death—the opposite of God's creative intention. As God sanctifies Christians, He tears down the high places in our lives—the things that represent rebellion and resistance—so that He can rebuild our hearts to love Him. Though His discipline seems harsh, it's evidence that He loves us and that He wants to restore beauty, order, and faith in our lives.

Jeremiah 5

*"It shall come about when they say, 'Why has the L*ord* our God done all these things to us?' then you shall say to them, 'As you have forsaken Me and served foreign gods in your land, so you will serve strangers in a land that is not yours.'"*   —*Jeremiah 5:19*

God doesn't create robots. After the Lord freed His people from slavery in Egypt and made a covenant with them at Sinai, He gave them the freedom either to obey Him or to forget His Law. Unfortunately, from the kings and priests all the way down to the citizens, they abandoned Him and brought foreign idols into His land. As a result of their misused freedom, God sent the Babylonian army to destroy the land and take His people captive. Their sin led them to bondage. God has given Christians the freedom and the power by the Spirit to obey Him or not. Even though Christ set us free from sin, we can still live as though sin has an unbreakable power over us. Thank God that in Christ we are bound by the law of grace (Romans 6:14–15). Let's use our freedom to obey Him.

Jeremiah 6

"Flee for safety, O sons of Benjamin,
From the midst of Jerusalem!
Now blow a trumpet in Tekoa
And raise a signal over Beth-haccerem;
For evil looks down from the north,
And a great destruction."   —*Jeremiah 6:1*

They could almost hear the horses' hooves pounding the ground and the troops shaking the earth as they charged. The inhabitants of Judah knew the dreaded Babylonians were coming—it was just a matter of time before they breached the city walls. Though the Lord could have wiped out His people without warning, He gave them ample opportunities to throw away their idols and return to Him. God sent prophet after prophet shouting, "Repent!" but His people closed their ears. God's warnings show His grace. The Lord won't send an army to attack Christians when we're disobedient. He will, however, refine the church and correct us when we're off track. Proverbs 3:11 says, "My child, don't reject the LORD's discipline, and don't be upset when he corrects you" (NLT). Are we skating on thin ice in our walk with the Lord, testing His grace? Let's heed God's Word out of gratitude for His patient grace.

Jeremiah 7

"Go now to My place which was in Shiloh, where I made My name dwell at the first, and see what I did to it because of the wickedness of My people Israel."   *—Jeremiah 7:12*

After the conquest of Canaan, Shiloh housed the ark of the covenant and attracted true worshipers (Joshua 18:1). But it didn't take long for holy Shiloh to turn into a house for idols. By the end of the era of the judges, idolatry had infiltrated God's tabernacle and evil had overtaken its priests (Judges 18:31; 1 Samuel 2:12–17). Just as God judged His people by the hand of the Philistines (1 Samuel 4:1–11), He would surely judge them for hundreds of years of idolatry, injustice, and insolence. The conqueror from the north was coming because God's people hadn't learned from their forefathers' sins and God's punishment. Just like Israel, we don't have to learn every lesson firsthand. God's inspired Word demonstrates how pride, idolatry, and injustice lead to destruction (1 Corinthians 10:6–11). We exercise wisdom when we learn from the examples of others in the pages of Scripture.

Jeremiah 8

"Were they ashamed because of the abomination they had done?
They certainly were not ashamed,
And they did not know how to blush;
Therefore they shall fall among those who fall;
At the time of their punishment they shall be brought down,"
Says the L*ORD*.   —*Jeremiah 8:12*

The people called by God's name had no boundaries when it
came to sin. They carved idols and bowed down to them. They
divorced their spouses on a whim. They even tied up their own
children and sacrificed them to demons. The inhabitants of
Judah had no shame. They had become so sophisticated in their
rebellion that they forgot how to blush. Unlike Judah, we must
not forget how to blush. We must not allow the voice of the Spirit
to go quiet in our lives. In our society, blushing and shame are
viewed as signs of the uptight, puritanical values of the past. As
believers, however, we must listen to the voice of the Spirit as He
guides us in holy living. We should follow the example of Joseph
who *ran away* when sin pursued him. When it comes to shame-
causing thoughts, God wants us to remain innocent and grow in
godly wisdom (Romans 16:19).

Jeremiah 9

"Their tongue is a deadly arrow;
It speaks deceit;
With his mouth one speaks peace to his neighbor,
But inwardly he sets an ambush for him."   —*Jeremiah 9:8*

God warned His people in Judah to practice discernment regarding the motives of one another. Why? Smooth talk slipped

across their lips while their hearts planned harm. Nothing could be further from God's character. The Lord has never spoken a deceitful word, nor has He slandered any person's character. Truth, integrity, and authenticity adorn His speech like the gold on a wedding band. God wants our words to resemble His, but He gives us the choice to use or abuse the powerful gift of communication. We would do well to consider our speech. Do our words reflect God's truth, or do we flatter others and malign their characters in secret? Do we gossip in the name of sharing prayer requests? Just as a switchblade can cause irreparable damage, our tongues can destroy others. Let's tame our tongues and speak truth (James 3:1–12).

Jeremiah 10

The portion of Jacob is not like these;
For the Maker of all is He,
And Israel is the tribe of His inheritance;
The Lord of Hosts is His name.   —*Jeremiah 10:16*

Worship is the only right response to God, and Jeremiah 10 explains why. The Lord is the ruler of all nations. He created all things by His wisdom. God has ultimate power to accomplish His plans. And He commands innumerable heavenly warriors to protect His people and execute judgment. So why didn't the people of Judah worship Him? They cared more about following what was "in style" than following their Lord. The nations that surrounded God's people constantly tempted them to abandon wisdom to pursue what was fashionable. Unfortunately, what was in vogue during Jeremiah's time provoked God's judgment. Today, it's not much different. When the sophisticated people of our culture call Christians simpletons for worshiping the Lord, remember Jeremiah 10. Though our culture doesn't worship gods of wood and stone, many sacrifice themselves to money, prestige, physical appearance, science, and immoral lifestyles in the name of progress. Remember: it's unwise *not* to worship God (Jeremiah 10:8).

Jeremiah 11

And the Lord said to me, "Proclaim all these words in the cities of Judah and in the streets of Jerusalem, saying, 'Hear the words of this covenant and do them.'" —*Jeremiah 11:6*

They treated the covenant like worthless, dirty garbage. Judah had violated God's Law and was about to reap the consequences. The Mosaic Covenant was a *temporary* arrangement that outlined the relationship between God and His people. In regard to the Mosaic Covenant, blessings would follow obedience, and curses would follow disobedience. But God's covenant with Abraham was an *eternal* promise of blessing, descendants, and land. Though God's people had cheated on their heavenly husband and would face His punishment, God would never violate His covenants. The Lord did inflict curses when His people disobeyed the Mosaic Covenant. Likewise, God will continue to carry out the eternal blessings of His covenant with Abraham. God keeps His promises even if we break faith. As His image bearers, the Lord wants us to keep our commitments with one another and follow through on our yeses and noes (James 5:12). Let's ask ourselves: Do we keep our word? Can others rely on us to keep our promises?

Jeremiah 12

"And it will come about that after I have uprooted them, I will again have compassion on them; and I will bring them back, each one to his inheritance and each one to his land."   *—Jeremiah 12:15*

Jeremiah roamed the streets of Jerusalem looking for signs of hope, but he found only rebellion and shame. As God's preacher of impending doom, Jeremiah told the people of Judah that their time had come—the Babylonian army was on its way. The sorrow of his message weighed heavily on Jeremiah. But he did have hope. God promised to have compassion on His people and to bring them back to the land they had poisoned with their spiritual adultery. Maybe the tune of Psalm 30:5 played in Jeremiah's heart: "For His anger is but for a moment, / His favor is for a lifetime." Many of us have friends or family members who are true believers but have strayed from the faith. Some have wandered farther than others. Though we pray for them and share with them God's truth, and they refuse to listen, we can hope that someday the Lord will bring them back so they can experience His grace.

Jeremiah 13

"This wicked people, who refuse to listen to My words, who walk in the stubbornness of their hearts and have gone after other gods to serve them and to bow down to them, let them be just like this waistband which is totally worthless."   *—Jeremiah 13:10*

God told Jeremiah to do some pretty crazy things—like putting on a loincloth (waistband), walking to the Spring of Perath, and shoving the loincloth in the crevices of the rocks. Later, God told Jeremiah to retrieve the cloth, which had become rotten.

The ruined, good-for-nothing loincloth illustrated the effect of Judah's pride. God's people had wandered from Him, blazed their own trail of disobedience, and had become like Jeremiah's loincloth—rotten, withered, and unable to fulfill its purpose. Instead of going their own way, the people of Judah should have clung to their God just as a useful loincloth clings to the one wearing it. Like Judah and the worthless loincloth, pride makes us good for nothing. Only those who follow the Lord and heed His commands will find joy and fulfill their purpose. As Christians, we must continually turn away from pride and abide in Christ in order to be useful in God's kingdom (John 15:4–5).

Jeremiah 14

Then the Lord said to me, "The prophets are prophesying falsehood in My name. I have neither sent them nor commanded them nor spoken to them; they are prophesying to you a false vision, divination, futility and the deception of their own minds."   *—Jeremiah 14:14*

From the beginning, false prophets have tried to twist God's Word and pull people away from Him. Their lies come straight from the first liar, Satan himself. Starting with the deception in the garden of Eden, false prophets distorted God's covenant and denied God's justice. They proclaimed peace and prosperity for the people of Judah while judgment waited outside the door. These deceitful teachers misread God's covenant with Moses and taught that idolatry would result in blessing. They only cared about their reputation and disregarded what God thought of them. The same is true today. Modern-day false prophets misinterpret God's Word and twist His promises, all for the sake of ratings. So what's the easiest way to spot these devious teachers? Listen to the apostle John:

"By this you know the Spirit of God: every spirit that confesses that Jesus Christ has come in the flesh is from God" (1 John 4:2). False teachers deny the deity of our Lord.

Jeremiah 15

Your words were found and I ate them,
And Your words became for me a joy and the delight of my heart;
For I have been called by Your name,
O Lord God of hosts. —Jeremiah 15:16

Bloodied and bruised, Jeremiah could barely stand under the weight of persecution, sorrow, and rejection. God's prophet even lamented his own birth (Jeremiah 15:10). Not only did he face depression within, Jeremiah watched as his own people rejected the Lord. All he could do was wait as God's judgment — personified in the Babylonian army — marched closer and closer to Jerusalem. Surrounded by moral, spiritual, and physical destruction, Jeremiah had nothing to cling to except God's Word. So Jeremiah consumed God's Word and found strength to face whatever God had planned. Jeremiah looked back on God's divine calling and rested in God's sovereignty. As the Lord of heaven's armies, God had angelic troops to defend Jeremiah (2 Kings 6:16–17). Like Jeremiah, we all face trials that make us feel hopeless. Where should we turn when waves of depression and disappointment threaten to capsize us? Only God's Word can give us hope, prove His love, and remind us of our identity in Christ.

Jeremiah 16

"You shall not take a wife for yourself nor have sons or daughters in this place." —*Jeremiah 16:2*

In a society where lifelong singleness and childlessness were viewed as evidence of divine judgment, God didn't allow Jeremiah to get married. Though Jeremiah lived a holy life, God asked him to walk this difficult path and reap the ridicule of others. As Jeremiah traveled his prophetic journey, weeping as he went, a wife and children would have provided much needed reassurance. Instead, Jeremiah had only God to comfort and console him. In New Testament times, the apostle Paul also lived with an ailment that God refused to remedy. But in Paul's pain, the Lord made him sufficient to fulfill His calling on Paul's life (2 Corinthians 12:6–10). Our sovereign God may ask some to take on trying tasks while others live in apparent ease. What if God asks us to forego comfort for His eternal purpose? Are we willing to give up our own plans for the sake of His glory?

Jeremiah 17

Thus says the LORD,
"Cursed is the man who trusts in mankind
And makes flesh his strength,
And whose heart turns away from the LORD." —*Jeremiah 17:5*

The people of Judah had a history of trusting in stronger nations in order to find security. They allied themselves with Egypt hoping that Egypt could provide the military backing Judah would need against Babylon (Ezekiel 29:16). Judah also trusted in idols to supply good crops and safety from invaders (Jeremiah 44:16–18). But Egypt and foreign gods couldn't provide ultimate security—nothing in our world system can.

Nevertheless, we tend to go to great lengths to feel safe. We seek impressive careers, admirable educational degrees, the right relationships, big bank accounts, and so on. But when we run to human-made sources of security, our hearts wander from the Lord. And when we don't soak our minds in God's Word and prayer, anxiety can take over. While Judah worried about invaders, worry doesn't have to seize our hearts. Through prayer and meditating on God's promises, we can find security in the midst of oppressing anxiety (Philippians 4:6–7).

Jeremiah 18

"At one moment I might speak concerning a nation or concerning a kingdom to uproot, to pull down, or to destroy it; if that nation against which I have spoken turns from its evil, I will relent concerning the calamity I planned to bring on it." —Jeremiah 18:7–8

God seems to wait until the very last minute to execute judgment, giving people plenty of time to repent. While the Israelites lived enslaved in Egypt for four hundred years, our long-suffering God gave the Amorites many opportunities to repent. When the Israelites escaped from Egypt and conquered the Promised Land, however, they killed the unrepentant Amorites and dispossessed them of their land. Their sin was "complete" (Genesis 15:16). And even when God's own people engaged in the most disgusting, idolatrous rituals, He sent Jeremiah with warnings and messages of forgiveness—if they would just repent. When we look at family, friends, and even nations who live corrupt lives but don't seem to face any consequences, remember that God is patient. In His grace, He gives people time to seek His forgiveness. And He wants us to tell others that the Lord is always ready to extend grace when someone repents—even to those who seem beyond forgiveness.

Jeremiah 19

"[They] have built the high places of Baal to burn their sons in the fire as burnt offerings to Baal, a thing which I never commanded or spoke of, nor did it ever enter My mind." —*Jeremiah 19:5*

To mistreat or kill the most innocent in our society—our children—is so foreign to God's character that it deserves the greatest punishment. In Judah, sin trickled from the top down, starting with King Manasseh, who burned his own son to the false god, Baal. By the time Jeremiah came along, Judah had gotten so entrenched in the evils of idolatry that they too sacrificed their own children to their "gods." They bound them and burned them alive—an act so barbaric that it repulsed God. Today, we can't even imagine committing such a heinous crime. We don't physically bind and burn our children as sacrifices, but we do sacrifice our children's welfare to the pursuit of money, prestige, selfish desires, and other idols. We also sacrifice many children in their mothers' wombs for selfish reasons. If we don't protect, care for, and prioritize the children in our lives and in our society, we deserve God's discipline.

Jeremiah 20

O Lord, You have deceived me and I was deceived;
You have overcome me and prevailed.
I have become a laughingstock all day long;
Everyone mocks me. —*Jeremiah 20:7*

Ever wonder if God really has the best plans for His people? Jeremiah did. He wondered if God had played a trick on him and deceived him into becoming a prophet. Jeremiah had received such harsh persecution that it caused him to question God's calling on his life. False teachers outnumbered God's true prophet, and Jeremiah's message of judgment didn't win him any friends. God's plan for us is to make His glory known, not to make sure we're happy all the time. Sometimes we find ourselves in the middle of a storm and begin wondering how much more we can take. Perhaps the ministry God has called us to hasn't produced much fruit—which can plague us with doubt. If life is good, we should be prepared for coming challenges to our faith, so that when these challenges surely hit us, we won't question God's calling. Our job is to glorify God, not to measure our own effectiveness.

Jeremiah 21

"Please inquire of the LORD on our behalf, for Nebuchadnezzar king of Babylon is warring against us; perhaps the LORD will deal with us according to all His wonderful acts, so that the enemy will withdraw from us." —Jeremiah 21:2

Longing to hear a message of hope, King Zedekiah sent two messengers to Jeremiah asking the prophet to intercede so that God would stop King Nebuchadnezzar's troops in their tracks. King Zedekiah hoped to escape Babylon's wrath just like Hezekiah had escaped Assyria's (2 Kings 19). But God said no. It was too late. Nothing could stop King Nebuchadnezzar because Babylon was God's instrument of judgment against His people. But Zedekiah and the people didn't want to hear that message. Today, many people want to hear the message of God's love, but they close their ears to the Bible's message of God's wrath. Like Jeremiah, when we tell others about God, we must paint a complete biblical picture of His character that includes both His grace as well as His anger over sin. Christians must also use discernment when listening to messages about God to make sure they reveal the whole story.

Jeremiah 22

"I spoke to you in your prosperity;
But you said, 'I will not listen!'
This has been your practice from your youth,
That you have not obeyed My voice."   —*Jeremiah 22:21*

The Lord had warned them but they refused to listen. And when their crops flourished and the vines bent over, heavy with fruit, they forgot God. During the reigns of King David and King Solomon, the Israelites experienced prosperity and political stability. In their wealth, pride swelled. It seemed that with each succeeding king, God's people wandered farther away from Him. The Israelites worshiped the idols of their neighbors, their priests twisted God's Law, and their officials neglected the poor and the needy. As a result of their arrogance, the Lord used Babylon to humiliate His people and kick them out of the Land of Promise. If we're not careful, prosperity can pull us away from God. We have to continually search our hearts when life is good—when we're healthy and wealthy—and make sure we're still dependent on and obedient to God. Pride and self-reliance tend to creep in when things are going well.

Jeremiah 23

"Behold, the days are coming," declares the LORD,
"When I will raise up for David a righteous Branch;
And He will reign as king and act wisely
And do justice and righteousness in the land."   —*Jeremiah 23:5*

In the midst of impending judgment, famine, destruction, and captivity, God shined the light of hope. Though the Lord planned to reckon as childless Jeconiah the son of Jehoiakim, king of Judah, the true King was coming (Jeremiah 22:24–30). After the Lord had judged the wicked shepherds of His people, He promised that a righteous Leader would sit on David's throne forever. The righteous Branch will one day gather the remnant of God's people from all the lands to which they were sent as captives. He will bring them back to their land as a united nation (Isaiah 11:11–12). Even though many Jews didn't recognize Messiah when He came the first time, He will come again. Like Jeconiah, our participation in the plan of God is a privilege, not a right. Although we can forfeit God using us to accomplish His plan, the plan cannot be thwarted.

Jeremiah 24

"I will make them a terror and an evil for all the kingdoms of the earth, as a reproach and a proverb, a taunt and a curse in all places where I will scatter them." —Jeremiah 24:9

When God disciplines His people, sometimes it causes a scene. Through Jeremiah, God reminded His people that when He judged them for their sin, everyone would notice. The other nations would walk by the smoking ruins of Jerusalem, shake their heads, and wonder how God's people had gone so wrong. Even for Christians, God's discipline sometimes causes a scene. Unfortunately, most people love a scandal—even inside the church. Instead of mourning over the fall of another church leader, do we secretly cheer? Does our pride revel in watching others fall? There's a part of us, deep in our sin nature, that finds comfort in knowing we're not as bad as the next guy. Or at least we're smart enough to not get caught. Be careful not to gossip the next time you hear about a church leader who has fallen. Instead, search your heart, confess pride, and pray for the fallen leader's restoration.

Jeremiah 25

"From the thirteenth year of Josiah the son of Amon, king of Judah, even to this day, these twenty-three years the word of the LORD has come to me, and I have spoken to you again and again, but you have not listened." —Jeremiah 25:3

How many of us would keep serving faithfully in a fruitless ministry for more than two decades? Many of us wouldn't last two years! Jeremiah served as God's prophet during the reigns of Josiah, Jehoiakim, and Zedekiah. By this point in his ministry, during the reign of Jehoiakim, Jeremiah had faithfully preached and prophesied for twenty-three years without any positive response. Not only did the people ignore Jeremiah's call to repentance, they tried to kill him (Jeremiah 11:18–23). Later, they would throw Jeremiah into a muddy, dark, cistern, leaving him for dead (38:6). But Jeremiah kept preaching because he trusted God's call on his life more than the response he had received from those to whom he preached. Jeremiah remembered that he served the eternal God who rules from heaven (25:30). Like Jeremiah, we should count as a privilege our service to the Lord regardless of the response we receive. So let's faithfully fulfill God's calling on our lives, trusting God with the results.

Jeremiah 26

When Jeremiah finished speaking all that the LORD had commanded him to speak to all the people, the priests and the prophets and all the people seized him, saying, "You must die!" —Jeremiah 26:8

It was a day like any other day. The priests, prophets, and the people went to the temple to carry out their religious duties. When they got there, Jeremiah was waiting with God's message to turn away from idolatry and injustice and seek God's mercy before it's too late. After Jeremiah finished preaching, the prophets and priests grabbed Jeremiah, put him on trial, and called for the death penalty. Of all the people, the religious elite harbored the most resentment against Jeremiah. They didn't recognize that God's true messenger was standing right in front of them. Even though churchgoing people serve as ministry leaders doesn't always mean that they have godly discernment or speak God's true message. We must sift through the filter of Scripture everything we hear from the religious leaders of our day. We must read God's Word and ask the Holy Spirit to help us develop discernment to recognize truth from error.

Jeremiah 27

"Now I have given all these lands into the hand of Nebuchadnezzar king of Babylon, My servant, and I have given him also the wild animals of the field to serve him." —Jeremiah 27:6

How could God call a pagan king His servant? The imperialist King Nebuchadnezzar of Babylon sought to expand his kingdom. Like a rushing river overflowing its banks, his army surged through the ancient Near East engulfing parts of modern-day Turkey, Iraq, Syria, Israel, Jordan, and Egypt. Can someone be God's instrument without knowing it? Back then and today, our sovereign Lord uses even unbelieving leaders to accomplish His will. As the supreme King—while allowing kings and political leaders to make their own decisions—He directs their hearts to achieve His will (Proverbs 21:1). When leaders we don't like take office, we can still trust that God is in control. Remember: "He controls the course of world events; / he removes kings and sets up other kings" (Daniel 2:21 NLT). Christians must respect their leaders even if they don't agree with their policies. God has given them positions of power, and He will use these leaders for His purposes.

Jeremiah 28

Hananiah spoke in the presence of all the people, saying, "Thus says the LORD, 'Even so will I break within two full years the yoke of Nebuchadnezzar king of Babylon from the neck of all the nations.'" Then the prophet Jeremiah went his way. —*Jeremiah 28:11*

Hananiah had nerve. He thought he could put words into God's mouth and mock His prophet, Jeremiah, without repercussion. Even in the face of false prophecy and ridicule, Jeremiah didn't let his anger get the best of him. When Hananiah proclaimed that the captives would return from Babylon in two short years, Jeremiah spoke the true words of the Lord (Jeremiah 28:7–9). And when Hananiah saw that Jeremiah didn't support his prophesy, Hananiah resorted to violence. Hananiah grabbed the yoke that Jeremiah had been wearing to show Judah's fate and broke it into pieces. Jeremiah, however, refused to stoop to Hananiah's use of force and instead walked away. Jeremiah didn't hurl insults at the false prophet but waited patiently for the Lord to deal with Hananiah. Likewise, when we are insulted for our faith or our obedience to God, we shouldn't respond with anger. Instead, we should wait for God's justice.

Jeremiah 29

"Seek the welfare of the city where I have sent you into exile, and pray to the LORD on its behalf; for in its welfare you will have welfare."   —*Jeremiah 29:7*

According to Jeremiah's prophecy, God's people would be in Babylon for a while (Jeremiah 29:10). For seventy years they would have to submit to a foreign king and live in a strange place with an unfamiliar language. But God told His exiles to get married and have kids, to plant gardens and reap their produce, and to build new lives in Babylon. Just as the Israelites lived as foreigners in Babylon, we should live as resident aliens wherever we are and abstain from the lusts that bring down those around us (1 Peter 2:11). We should seek the welfare of our cities and nation, praying for wisdom for our leaders so that we can all live in security and peace. And it shouldn't stop there. If we struggle to get along with a coworker or family member, let's pray for God's blessing and pursue peace in our relationships (Romans 12:18).

Jeremiah 30

"Thus says the LORD, the God of Israel, 'Write all the words which I have spoken to you in a book.'"   —*Jeremiah 30:2*

The Lord told Jeremiah to write his prophecies in a book in order to keep an inspired record of God's faithfulness. Then, when God kept His promises, His people could look back and read of Jeremiah's prophecies and their perfect fulfillments. Jeremiah's scroll would also serve as a witness against those who had rejected God's words through His prophets. In His grace, the Lord has given us the Bible, a record of His redemptive plan throughout history, so that we can live with hope. In fact, God's Word is even more dependable than the natural laws of the universe (Jeremiah 31:36). Do we trust God's promises in His Word as much as we trust in gravity or the rising and setting sun? Let's examine our hearts. Do we put more faith in the opinions of others, our own feelings, or some other unreliable thing than we do the inerrant, fully reliable truth of God's Word?

Jeremiah 31

"Again I will build you and you will be rebuilt,
O virgin of Israel!
Again you will take up your tambourines,
And go forth to the dances of the merrymakers."   —*Jeremiah 31:4*

Though God's people faced His burning anger for their idolatry, He promised to one day bring all the exiles back into the Promised Land. God even called Israel His *virgin* because His grace will one day restore the nation's innocence. On that future day, the Lord will replace hopelessness with joy. His people will pick up their tambourines and sing of God's grace. And where the enemy had made the land barren, God's people will harvest crops and live in peace. As Christians who struggle against our sin nature, we still disobey God. But when guilt weighs us down, we must remember that God sees us through Christ's righteousness afforded to us through His life, death, and resurrection. If bad choices have taken away our innocence, Christ's forgiveness can make us pure again and restore joy. And just as God forgives His rebellious people, we should likewise extend God's grace to others.

Jeremiah 32

"They have turned their back to Me and not their face; though I taught them, teaching again and again, they would not listen and receive instruction." —*Jeremiah 32:33*

When a defiant teenager wants to show disrespect to his or her parents, the teenager will turn around and walk away while his or her parents are still talking. But Judah wasn't a teenager anymore. God's people should have outgrown their juvenile ways long ago. After all they had experienced with God—from their deliverance from slavery, to God's miraculous provision in the wilderness and their occupation of the lush Land of Promise—God's people refused to grow up. They shirked God's discipline and like a defiant teenager, turned their backs on God. God the Father pursued the Israelites with messages of warning and grace, but they refused to turn back toward Him. We must not allow any areas of our lives to prevent us from turning back toward the Lord and asking for His blessing. Let's leave childish ways behind and discipline ourselves so that God won't have to.

Jeremiah 33

"Thus says the LORD of hosts, 'There will again be in this place which is waste, without man or beast, and in all its cities, a habitation of shepherds who rest their flocks.'" —*Jeremiah 33:12*

In the desolate, war-ravaged city of Jerusalem, where not even beasts could live, God promised to one day make it a place peaceful enough for shepherds to care for their flocks. At the hands of the cruel Babylonian army, many of God's people were lost. But under the future rule of the faithful Shepherd, life will be preserved (Jeremiah 33:16). The corrupt kings and priests of Israel who had led the nation into sin and judgment will be a distant memory. The Good Shepherd, the righteous Davidic King, will restore justice and genuine worship. As believers in the Good Shepherd, we have peace even in the midst of chaos, pain, and loss. When unrighteousness infiltrates our communities and our laws, we have hope in the Shepherd who will rule with perfect justice. Let's share the peace of Christ and our hope of resurrection with our friends who feel ravaged by tragedy and hopelessness.

Jeremiah 34

"You will not escape from his hand, for you will surely be captured and delivered into his hand; and you will see the king of Babylon eye to eye, and he will speak with you face to face, and you will go to Babylon." —Jeremiah 34:3

God takes our promises seriously. He held King Zedekiah accountable for rebelling against the king of Babylon and breaking their covenant (Ezekiel 17:11–21). Zedekiah had become Babylon's vassal, sworn loyalty to King Nebuchadnezzar, and then turned to Egypt for military help to betray Nebuchadnezzar. Knowing Zedekiah's track record of broken commitments, God sent Jeremiah to encourage him to surrender to Nebuchadnezzar. With the Babylonian troops at Jerusalem's door, Zedekiah had a choice—trust in God's protection and keep faith with Nebuchadnezzar or rebel, *again*. Zedekiah tried to escape, but the Babylonian officials caught him and gouged out his eyes. Zedekiah's rebellion met with harsh consequences. But even though Zedekiah broke faith, God still kept His promise to let

Zedekiah die in peace rather than in battle (Jeremiah 52:11). How many commitments have we broken, both with God and with others, and God still shows us grace? Even though we're faithless, God always remains faithful (2 Timothy 2:13).

Jeremiah 35

"And do not build houses or plant crops or vineyards, but always live in tents. If you follow these commands, you will live long, good lives in the land." —*Jeremiah 35:7 NLT*

The Recabites made difficult choices in order to follow their fathers' commands not to drink wine, build houses, or plant crops. They denied themselves comfort and lived as nomads. Even when God's prophet, Jeremiah, served them wine, they refused to drink it. If the Recabites disciplined themselves to follow their earthly fathers' commands, how much more should Christians discipline themselves to follow their heavenly Father's commands? God's goal for our lives is godliness—and it takes discipline on our part to achieve that goal (1 Timothy 4:7–8). Christ modeled the disciplined life, completely surrendered to His Father. Do we live with the self-restraint of a soldier or with the laziness of a couch potato? How much time could we redirect from the TV, computer, or smartphones to prayer, Bible study, or fellowship? Are we willing to give up some comfort in order to incorporate the spiritual disciplines into our lives?

Jeremiah 36

Yet the king and all his servants who heard all these words were not afraid, nor did they rend their garments. —*Jeremiah 36:24*

Zedekiah and his officials sat stone-faced as Baruch read Jeremiah's words from the scroll. They didn't feel remorse at the record of their sins, and they didn't tremble at the Lord's anger. Like a paraplegic who has lost all feeling in his or her legs, the king and his princes had lost their capacity to feel God convicting their hearts. Not only had the king grown cold toward God, he burned Jeremiah's scroll as a declaration of defiance against God. We may not act so blatantly defiant as to burn our Bibles, but do we truly fear the Lord? Do we make it our priority to revere and obey Him? Christians hear about God's wrath and grace so much that sometimes we lose our sensitivity to our own sin. Have we lost our ability to sense the Holy Spirit's conviction? Or do we try to convince ourselves that certain Bible verses don't apply to us?

Jeremiah 37

"For even if you had defeated the entire army of Chaldeans who were fighting against you, and there were only wounded men left among them, each man in his tent, they would rise up and burn this city with fire." —*Jeremiah 37:10*

The destruction of Jerusalem was set in stone by the Lord. He had preordained to judge His people, and no one could stand in His way. Even if the Israelites wounded the entire Babylonian army, the Babylonians would still overthrow Jerusalem and take God's people captive. Why? Because unlike His people, God keeps His covenant promises. In the Mosaic Law, God promised certain curses if the Israelites abandoned Him for idols and treated His Law as worthless. The Lord knew exactly what it would take to humble His people and bring them back to Him. Like a wise Father, God uses perfect discipline to appropriately deal with sin. Only the Lord knows what it will take to break us of certain sins. Though we no longer live under the Mosaic Law, God still demands obedience to His Word. As a perfect Father, He loves us enough to discipline us appropriately to fit our offense . . . all to bring us back to obedience.

Jeremiah 38

Then Ebed-melech the Ethiopian said to Jeremiah, "Now put these worn-out clothes and rags under your armpits under the ropes"; and Jeremiah did so.   —Jeremiah 38:12

The compassion and faith of a foreigner saved Jeremiah's life. Ebed-melech, an Ethiopian official in King Zedekiah's regime, had the courage to defy the other officials who wanted to kill Jeremiah. After hearing one more of Jeremiah's sermons telling God's people to surrender to the Babylonian king, King Zedekiah's officials threw Jeremiah into a cistern and left him for dead. But Ebed-melech had compassion on Jeremiah, so he went to King Zedekiah and appealed for Jeremiah's life. With the help of thirty men, Ebed-melech rescued Jeremiah from the cistern that would have become his tomb. Knowing how weak Jeremiah was, Ebed-melech got some old rags to add cushion to the ropes that would have caused Jeremiah extra pain. Because of Ebed-melech's faith and kindness to Jeremiah, the Lord promised to protect Ebed-melech from the invading Babylonians (Jeremiah 39:16–18). When believers show kindness to someone in distress, they demonstrate God's grace which pleases Him.

Jeremiah 39

*He then blinded Zedekiah's eyes and bound him in fetters of bronze
to bring him to Babylon.* —Jeremiah 39:7

After almost two years of battle, the enemy finally penetrated the wall surrounding the holy city. When the rival king and his officials took control of Jerusalem, King Zedekiah had a choice — obey God's counterintuitive instructions and remain in the city or flee for his life. He chose to run away from King Nebuchadnezzar and away from God. The Lord had commanded Zedekiah to surrender to the king of Babylon, but instead, Zedekiah, his sons, and his officials tried to escape. But Nebuchadnezzar caught Zedekiah and his entourage, killed everyone before Zedekiah's eyes, and gouged out Zedekiah's eyes. Disobedience always leads to spiritual blindness. If we have trouble finding God's will or viewing our lives from His perspective, we must examine our hearts. Is there disobedience there? Have we gotten into the habit of questioning God's sometimes seemingly counterintuitive instructions for our lives, following our own will instead? Maybe it's time we reexamine Romans 12:1–2.

Jeremiah 40

*Then Jeremiah went to Mizpah to Gedaliah the son of Ahikam and
stayed with him among the people who were left in the land.*
—Jeremiah 40:6

True love is hard to kill. Jeremiah loved his people and the land of God's eternal promises. After the fall of Jerusalem, Nebuzaradan, the captain of King Nebuchadnezzar's bodyguard, gave Jeremiah the choice to stay in Judah or go to Babylon. Though many of his own people had tried to kill him, Jeremiah chose to stay in

Judah. As God's prophet, Jeremiah knew that the Lord had great plans for His people and His land. The judgment they faced didn't mean the end of their existence as a people. At the perfect time, God would call to His exiled people and bring them back. But in the meantime, Jeremiah stayed to encourage and inspire hope in those who lingered in the devastated land. Jeremiah's commitment to God's plan of restoration should inspire us to seek restoration in our broken relationships. Just as love caused Jeremiah to stay, love should push us to seek reconciliation.

Jeremiah 41

Ishmael left Mizpah to meet them, weeping as he went. When he reached them, he said, "Oh, come and see what has happened to Gedaliah!" —Jeremiah 41:6 NLT

Ishmael, the coldhearted killer, lured the broken pilgrims into Mizpah to slaughter them. He used deceit and trickery and played on their emotions to trick them. And after Ishmael had slaughtered them, he denied them the respect of a burial and dumped their lifeless bodies into a cistern. The cistern Ishmael chose was the one King Asa had dug in order to provide water for his people as they battled King Basha of Israel (Jeremiah 41:9). Ishmael turned a life-giving cistern into a tomb. That's exactly what Satan does. He steals life and gives death in return. The Evil One twists the desires God intends for good—for love, comfort, provision, and other good things—and makes them evil. Satan uses sleight of hand to deceive us, giving evil the appearance of good. We should use discernment when making decisions and putting our trust in the people and the things of this world.

Jeremiah 42

For you have only deceived yourselves; for it is you who sent me to the LORD your God, saying, "Pray for us to the LORD our God; and whatever the LORD our God says, tell us so, and we will do it."
                                                        —Jeremiah 42:20

Johanan and his fellow military leaders asked Jeremiah to pray for God's guidance as to whether they should stay in Jerusalem or go to Egypt. They vowed to obey whatever the Lord told them to do. But they were lying. Though they had the appearance of humility and compliance, really they just wanted God to endorse their plan to go to Egypt. So when Jeremiah told them to stay in Jerusalem and submit to the Babylonians, they left. And they paid the price with their lives. There are consequences when our prayers to God don't display a genuine desire to follow God's will. Sometimes we just want His stamp of approval on *our* plans. Instead, we should pray like Jesus, who laid down His own agenda to follow His Father's will. What areas of our lives are we unwilling to submit to God's superior plan?

Jeremiah 43

So Johanan the son of Kareah and all the commanders of the forces, and all the people, did not obey the voice of the LORD to stay in the land of Judah.   *—Jeremiah 43:4*

Johanan and the leaders in Jerusalem asked Jeremiah to seek God's guidance for them and promised to obey. But when Jeremiah told them God's instructions to stay in Judah, they refused to obey because they didn't like what they heard. Johanan and some of the remaining Jews left for Egypt. Sometimes we only hear what we want to hear from the Lord. As sinners, we all have the tendency to manipulate the Bible to say what we want to hear. And sometimes we lead others astray when we share our twisted theology. People like messages that tickle their ears and stroke their egos (2 Timothy 4:3). Some of the biggest churches spout warped doctrine and alter the truths of Scripture to make it more palatable . . . and people flock to these churches. Do our souls desire the pure milk of the Word? And do we communicate to others the truth of God's Word?

Jeremiah 44

"But they did not listen or incline their ears to turn from their wickedness, so as not to burn sacrifices to other gods." —*Jeremiah 44:5*

God's people wore spiritual earplugs. Prophet after prophet gave them specific instructions to keep them in God's will but they wouldn't listen. Now, with the remnant living in Egypt in defiance of God's command to stay in Judah, all they could do was await His judgment—*again*. For centuries, God's people refused to incline their ears and their hearts to their Lord. But what does it mean to incline our ears to God? The Hebrew word for "incline" pictures someone leaning close with anticipation to hear *and obey* every word. To incline our ears to God requires soft hearts and humility (Jeremiah 44:10). We can look to God as our model. He inclines His ear to our prayers, listens intently, and responds. Do we seek God's guidance for large and small concerns and then listen expectantly with the intention to obey? As we read God's Word and seek His will in prayer, let's incline our ears and our hearts to Him.

Jeremiah 45

"'But you, are you seeking great things for yourself? Do not seek them; for behold, I am going to bring disaster on all flesh,' declares the Lord, 'but I will give your life to you as booty in all the places where you may go.'" —Jeremiah 45:5

Our culture taunts us with hopes of comfort and ease, promising we can get rich quick and evade the sometimes grueling responsibilities of life. Baruch, Jeremiah's scribe, zigzagged through the devastated streets of Jerusalem, as he and Jeremiah shared God's message of judgment. One day, weary under his heavy load of grief, Baruch complained to God because Jerusalem lay desolate while God's people suffered in exile (Jeremiah 45:3). But the Lord didn't slap Baruch on the hand for complaining. Instead, He extended grace and reminded Baruch that in the midst of judgment, God had preserved Baruch's life. God's grace shines brightest in the midst of trials that highlight our need for Him. In comfort and ease, we're tempted to disregard God and rely on ourselves. God's words to Baruch remind us that life, even when accompanied by suffering, is a gracious gift. Each day presents a new chance to participate in God's plan of redemption.

Jeremiah 46

For that day belongs to the Lord GOD of hosts,
A day of vengeance, so as to avenge Himself on His foes;
And the sword will devour and be satiated
And drink its fill of their blood;
For there will be a slaughter for the Lord GOD of hosts,
In the land of the north by the river Euphrates. —Jeremiah 46:10

Nations build up armies and multiply weapons to defend their sovereignty and to defeat their enemies. Judah's military had fought hard against the Babylonian forces and lost because the Lord of heaven's armies had decreed Judah's destruction. When the shell-shocked group of Jews fled to Egypt, they expected to find peace in a well-protected country. Unfortunately, the Lord of Hosts had already planned to overwhelm the Egyptian army in judgment for Egypt's idolatry. When we read through the Old Testament, we can almost trace God's hand through the military battles between God's people and their neighboring nations. That's because God, the commander-in-chief of the angelic armies, exercised complete, sovereign control over His people. And He still does today. Though we don't live in a theocracy like Israel did, God still sends His angels to defend Christians. Often, however, we don't take seriously His protection and His desire to respond to our prayers for help.

Jeremiah 47

"Ah, sword of the Lord,
How long will you not be quiet?
Withdraw into your sheath;
Be at rest and stay still."   —*Jeremiah 47:6*

Jeremiah lived in an era of judgment. The prophet longed for a time when the Lord would put away His sword and when His grace would rule. But until God's sword accomplished His judgment against His people and against the wicked nations, it would keep cutting down the proud (Jeremiah 47:7). From Israel and Judah to Assyria, Babylon, and Egypt, the Lord poured out His wrath. But Jeremiah had seen enough carnage. He longed for peace. Today we live in an era of grace. Wickedness runs wild and the tide of injustice seems to have come in. We wonder why God seems silent and doesn't deal with sin. But we forget that Jesus will one day brandish His sword and take care of injustice (Revelation 19:11–16). After the final judgment, the Lord will throw away His sword forever and the era of everlasting peace will dawn. Until then, God wants people to repent.

Jeremiah 48

"So gladness and joy are taken away
From the fruitful field, even from the land of Moab.
And I have made the wine to cease from the wine presses;
No one will tread them with shouting,
The shouting will not be shouts of joy."   —Jeremiah 48:33

Screams of sorrow had replaced shouts of joy in Moab. When God judged Moab for its complacency, pride, and idolatry, He promised to remove all the things that gave that nation joy. One of Moab's greatest sources of joy was its fruitful land that produced delicious grapes and renowned wine. But God's judgment through the conquest of Babylon would destroy the fruitful land and take away Moab's joy. Joy comes from the Lord, and it should characterize the life of a believer. But Christians shouldn't find their chief joy in their paychecks, their lifestyles, and other things that provide temporary fulfillment. Just like the fruitful land of Moab faced devastation, any source of joy other than God will inevitably disappoint us. The Lord has already given us joy, and we must choose to walk in joy whether or not our vines are producing abundant crops (Philippians 4:4).

Jeremiah 49

"Leave your orphans behind, I will keep them alive;
And let your widows trust in Me."   *—Jeremiah 49:11*

In a book full of war and God's wrath, we see glimpses of His tender heart. While most of God's people were exiled to Babylon, the poorest remained in Judah. The Babylonian forces took the best and the brightest Hebrews (Daniel 1:3–5) and left behind the orphans and widows. Though everyone else discounted the orphans and widows, the Lord promised them protection and provision. Even in the midst of His wrath, God has a tender heart toward the forgotten and exploited. Do our hearts beat for those society leaves behind? Do we weep for abandoned children or forgotten widows? Do we reach out to the needy in our paths, even in our own families? If not, then our hearts don't resemble God's. The next time God gives us an opportunity to care for the orphans and widows in our society, let's jump in and get to know those whom the Lord loves so much.

Jeremiah 50

"My people have become lost sheep;
Their shepherds have led them astray.
They have made them turn aside on the mountains;
They have gone along from mountain to hill
And have forgotten their resting place."   *—Jeremiah 50:6*

Judah's bad shepherds—their priests and false prophets—led God's people astray. Many practiced false religions and encouraged idolatry. Instead of reminding the people about God's promises, grace, and justice, they led the people in shallow feasts and perfunctory worship services. These bad shepherds gathered all of God's people and led them away from God—like sheep being led into the barren wilderness with no food, water, or protection and left to die. God holds people accountable who exercise spiritual authority over others. Those of us who serve as pastors, church leaders, lay teachers, parents, and others in positions of spiritual authority should make sure we're leading the sheep closer to God. We should examine our words about God, our actions, whether or not we live with integrity, and our commitment to spiritual disciplines. Just as God held accountable Judah's shepherds for leading their sheep away from the Lord, He will also hold us responsible.

Jeremiah 51

But the God of Israel is no idol!
He is the Creator of everything that exists,
including his people, his own special possession.
The Lord of Heaven's Armies is his name!

—Jeremiah 51:19 NLT

As we look back at Israel's history, it's hard to imagine how God's people—the chosen people; the object of God's affection; the recipients of miracles, prophets, and His direct communication—got so off track. The Lord delivered His people from slavery in the idol-worshiping nation of Egypt, gave them heavenly food and water in the wilderness, and showered on them wealth and beauty in Canaan. Israel's history demonstrates God's love. But by Jeremiah's day, God's people had gone so far astray that they bowed down to carved rocks. Why? God's people forgot that He is the Creator of everything! Before the first speck of dust floated in the universe, Father, Son, and Spirit existed. Legions of angels were at His beck-and-call. The first human beings, Adam and Eve, bore His image and revealed His love. May we never forget to honor God as God. May we never treat the Creator as a mere creature.

Jeremiah 52

But Nebuzaradan the captain of the guard left some of the poorest of the land to be vinedressers and plowmen. —Jeremiah 52:16

God protected the poorest of the land by causing Babylon to leave them in Judah. Though He had kicked out from the land of Judah most of His people, God gave these impoverished Israelites a responsibility in the land to tend the crops and plow the fields. The Lord provided the poor with food, work, and purpose. Though the land of Judah had been forsaken by His people, who refused to give it Sabbath rest for 490 years, the poor inhabitants of Judah witnessed God's restoration of His land while most of His people lived as exiles in Babylon. God still cares for the poor, and He expects Christians with resources to meet the needs of the poor, both inside and outside the church walls. Even if we're not financially impoverished, we're *all* spiritually poor and in desperate need of salvation, spiritual nourishment, and purpose in life (Matthew 5:3).

Lamentations

Lamentations 1

How lonely sits the city
That was full of people! . . .
All her friends have dealt treacherously with her; . . .
Judah has gone into exile.   *—Lamentations 1:1–3*

In five chapters Jeremiah related five "lamentations," or songs of mourning. The weeping prophet introduced the theme of his book by stating that because Jerusalem had abandoned the Lord by pursing idols and foreign alliances, God had given over the city to the Babylonians, who disciplined Jerusalem by forcing most of its citizens into exile. The glorious city that once stood mighty among the nations now lay devastated, ruined by the very same idol-worshiping foreigners Jerusalem had befriended. Whether by natural consequences or by God's direct intervention, the principle of divine discipline always comes as an expression both of God's faithfulness and His love. He promises to bring reproof upon us when we fail to repent so that we might return to Him (Proverbs 1:23; 3:12). God intends the ruins of our regret to lead us to repentance, "for those whom the Lord loves He disciplines" (Hebrews 12:6). His reproof comes from the heart of a loving Father.

Lamentations 2

"Pour out your heart like water
Before the presence of the Lord;
Lift up your hands to Him
For the life of your little ones
Who are faint because of hunger."   —*Lamentations 2:19*

The most heartrending consequences of Judah's willful sins against God came as Jeremiah witnessed the children of the city starving as a result of the sins of those who came before them. Our selfish decisions and sins betray the priority of our hearts: *self*. Seldom do we consider that the fallout of our self-serving decisions can devastate our children's well-being for a lifetime. The consequences of our compromises hurt more than just us—much worse than we ever imagine. The results of our sins can harm those closest to us, and more than anyone, our children might find themselves caught up in a dire situation they had no part in creating. When we see children in such circumstances, we must respond with determined intercession. As Jeremiah urged: "Pour out your heart like water / Before the presence of the Lord . . . / For the life of your little ones" (Lamentations 2:19).

Lamentations 3

Why should any living mortal, or any man,
Offer complaint in view of his sins?
Let us examine and probe our ways,
And let us return to the Lord.   —*Lamentations 3:39–40*

God's kindness to us always comes on the basis of His grace—not justice. Why? Because God remains under no obligation to forgive our sins (apart from Christ)—only to judge them. If we suffer any hardship at all, it measures little against the weight of justice we deserve for our willful sins. And yet, even still, God offers mercy to the contrite of heart. Our hope for a future of mercy comes for one reason: "The LORD's lovingkindnesses indeed never cease, / For His compassions never fail. / They are new every morning" (Lamentations 3:22–23). One purpose of pain is to cause us to reflect on the effects of our sin. We should "examine and probe our ways" in order to gain perspective and motivation to change directions. The bitterness of our consequences draws us like a magnet to "return to the LORD." If we will come to Him, He will begin the process of restoration. We know He will because He said He would, and great is His faithfulness.

Lamentations 4

Yet our eyes failed,
Looking for help was useless;
In our watching we have watched
For a nation that could not save.   *—Lamentations 4:17*

Jeremiah's fourth lament contrasts Jerusalem's barrenness to the city's better condition before its desolation. Both sides of comparison point to the same application: Jerusalem's suffering represents God's discipline for the sins of its citizens. Judah had looked to Egypt to save them from the threat of Babylon, but Egypt proved unreliable and ineffective against the calamity God had ordained via Judah's enemies—a fact Jeremiah had told the king of Judah beforehand (Jeremiah 37:5–10). In moments of need, human help often seems preferable to relying on God . . . especially when people tell us what we want to hear, when they offer quick solutions as opposed to waiting on God, and when their advice seems an easy alternative to the sometimes hard choices faith demands. But when God's clear will points to trusting Him alone, we will always discover that our "looking for help [elsewhere] was useless." Sometimes God puts us in places where only He is the solution so we will learn to rely only on Him.

Lamentations 5

You, O Lord, rule forever;
Your throne is from generation to generation. . . .
Restore us to You, O Lord, that we may be restored;
Renew our days as of old. —*Lamentations 5:19, 21*

Rising from the fog of despair and lament, Jeremiah recorded Judah's prayer of hope. The Jews appealed to God's mercy based on their confidence in His sovereignty. If God's providence had caused Judah's downfall, then His mighty hand could also act on Judah's behalf to bring about the nation's restoration—only as God can restore. Because Judah's repentance was genuine, its citizens rested in the assurance that God would indeed act and not forget them (Leviticus 26:44; Jeremiah 31:31–37). Jeremiah's book of Lamentations ends with a message of hope based on the character of God and the promises of God—in spite of the sin of His people. In New Testament times, the apostle Paul urged Christians to take comfort that because God has not forsaken His promises to Israel in spite of their sin, neither would He forsake us Christians when we blow it (Romans 8:1, 35–39; 11:1–2). If God did not renege on His promises to Israel in view of their sin, what confidence can we Christians have that God will not forsake us in view of our own sins? His faithfulness to Israel mirrors His faithfulness to the church.

Ezekiel

Ezekiel 1

Now it came about in the thirtieth year, on the fifth day of the fourth month, while I was by the river Chebar among the exiles, the heavens were opened and I saw visions of God. —Ezekiel 1:1

We never know when our day will be transformed by the unexpected movement of God. Five years into the Babylonian captivity, the displaced people of Judah surely felt forgotten by God. Their exile was justified; God had warned His people of dire consequences if they were unfaithful to Him. Tantalized by foreign gods, the kingdom of Judah disregarded the Lord's warnings . . . and consequences came. Now stunned and purposeless, the Jews languished in a refugee camp down by the river and spent their days wondering if they had any hope or future. But God had not forgotten them, even in the midst of their disobedience, so He chose Ezekiel to communicate with them once more. Ezekiel listened to and looked for God, in spite of bleak circumstances. God never had to reassure Ezekiel to be unafraid, even as Ezekiel beheld unearthly, disturbing heavenly visions. Regardless of his circumstances, Ezekiel must have cultivated that capacity to hear from God and obey. God's love and care for Israel did not cease after their exile. God doesn't abandon His own, though He disciplines those He loves. He has not forgotten us in the midst of our mundane days, our extreme crises, or even our deserved discipline. Through God's Word, prayer, and the ministry of the Holy Spirit, the communication lines between God and us are always open.

Ezekiel 2

*"I am sending you to them who are stubborn and obstinate children,
and you shall say to them, 'Thus says the Lord G*OD*.'"* —*Ezekiel 2:4*

Children can be stubborn. Very, very stubborn. They won't put
away their toys. They refuse to eat the brussels sprouts. They
wrestle against holding their parents' hands while crossing the
street. Children, with all the energy and selfish focus they can
muster, vie to get their way. But often they don't have the benefit
of wisdom, experience, or the bigger picture. They don't always
know that their disobedience can have harmful consequences.
How much more do we rebel against the wisdom of God in order
to have our own shortsighted way? As Christians, we are called
to heed not our own understanding but to acknowledge God
in everything we do and say . . . to seek His hand in guiding us
across the gridlocked intersections of life and to point people to
His perspective. In a world that desires its own way, we are called
to say, "Thus says the Lord God," in hope that the world will
choose submission over stubbornness.

Ezekiel 3

*"However, if you have warned the righteous man that the righteous
should not sin and he does not sin, he shall surely live because he
took warning; and you have delivered yourself."* —*Ezekiel 3:21*

God appointed Ezekiel to obey a difficult task—to declare His
words to people who would reject them. God forewarned Ezekiel
that when given the words of life, the people would still choose
death. Disclaimer: We are *not* the Holy Spirit. God doesn't expect
us to win souls to Christ. After all, without the mercy and movement of God, we couldn't muster the faith to believe in salvation

through Jesus Christ. In our day, as in Ezekiel's day, God desires obedience and compassion—the ability to respond to the message of hope and conviction that God has given us in the gospel and the willingness to share it with a rebellious and utterly broken world. We are completely incapable of managing hearers' responses to God's message, so we mustn't try! All we can do is share the hope of life through belief in Jesus Christ. The worst thing we can do is hide our hope from those who languish in despair. Compassion keeps our sharing of the gospel humble and God-focused. When we are disgusted with the immorality of our neighbors, remember Christ's sacrificial love for them—and for us. We must allow compassion to compel us to obediently share the gospel with others. Who knows: God may honor us by allowing us to see His transforming work in someone we thought was beyond hope.

Ezekiel 4

"As for you, lie down on your left side and lay the iniquity of the house of Israel on it; you shall bear their iniquity for the number of days that you lie on it." —*Ezekiel 4:4*

It must have pained Ezekiel to lie on one side, to bake bread over fire made with dung, and to ration his water and bread as if he were in a famine, all for more than a year. His suffering was not a result of his own disobedience but a sign to his neighbors about God's mercy. God chose to warn His people in hope that they would repent before the coming siege. Witnessing to others can be costly. The price can be isolation from friends or family, lack of promotion or termination from a job. In some parts of the world, witnessing can lead to death. Remember, though, that what the

Lord asks of His followers is no less than God asked of His own Son, whose example we have the privilege of following: "Have this attitude in yourselves which was also in Christ Jesus . . . Being found in appearance as a man, He humbled Himself by becoming obedient to the point of death, even death on a cross" (Philippians 2:5, 8).

Ezekiel 5

"Thus says the Lord GOD, 'This is Jerusalem; I have set her at the center of the nations, with lands around her. But she has rebelled against My ordinances more wickedly than the nations and against My statutes more than the lands which surround her; for they have rejected My ordinances and have not walked in My statutes.'"

—*Ezekiel 5:5–6*

God bestowed upon the Israelite exiles privilege, safety, and wealth; but instead of glorifying Him, the people of Israel became arrogant. God loathes self-exaltation; therefore, we must be mindful of our need for humility in times of plenty and ease. We must acknowledge the goodness of God during times of prosperity. Every good gift comes from Him (James 1:17). In Him we have everything, and without Him we could not exist. We cannot comprehend—cannot even begin to fathom—the depths of mercy, forgiveness, sacrificial love, and safety wrapped up in the incarnation of Jesus Christ. God is holy and cannot tolerate sin. God is lovely and cannot commune with ugliness. The intent and actions of humankind are soiled and heavy with self-importance. It's wise to remember that God opposes the proud but exalts the humble (1 Peter 5:5).

Ezekiel 6

"Then you will know that I am the Lord, when their slain are among their idols around their altars, on every high hill, on all the tops of the mountains, under every green tree and under every leafy oak—the places where they offered soothing aroma to all their idols."

—*Ezekiel 6:13*

Sometimes we can have trouble reconciling the God who declares His sovereignty through His wrathful slaying of those who sin against Him and the God who declares His sovereignty through His loving sacrifice of His Son. The Bible assures us that Jesus, the healer and reconciler who laid down His life for us, is the perfect, incarnate representation of the same God full of wrath in Ezekiel 6. The bridge to reconciling these two seemingly disparate portraits is *holiness*. God is utterly holy. Those who sin must atone and repent or be punished. The house of Israel chose rebellion, and a holy God responded. Yet, even in His white-hot wrath, God promised to preserve a remnant—a strand of mercy in the face of destruction. In the New Testament, God's holiness did not change, but the thread of mercy extended and widened under the perfect atonement found in Christ's substitutionary sacrifice on the cross. He did what we could not do for ourselves. If we believe, His atonement covers us once and for all.

Ezekiel 7

"They transformed the beauty of His ornaments into pride, and they made the images of their abominations and their detestable things with it; therefore I will make it an abhorrent thing to them. I will give it into the hands of the foreigners as plunder and to the wicked of the earth as spoil, and they will profane it." —Ezekiel 7:20–21

In Ezekiel 7, part of God's punishment for Judah was that the temple be looted and profaned by foreigners. God's wrath wasn't directed at the looters but at the people who profaned the temple with their pride—namely, the Israelites. The people of God have no business misusing the things of God in order to glorify or puff up ourselves. Local churches are not playgrounds for the egos of men, and God will not be mocked. Thankfully, though, when people, whether inside or outside of the believing community, attempt to mock God through pride or disdain, He never changes. His glory is not tied to a building, a denomination, or a political party; it is unchanging, infinite, and eternal. Do you ever feel livid after reading about a church burning? Or want to jump to the defense of a wronged religious person or group? It's not disobedient to feel this righteous anger, and it's a comfort to know that attempts to smear the reputation of the living God are always, always in vain.

Ezekiel 8

Then He said to me, "Son of man, do you see what the elders of the house of Israel are committing in the dark, each man in the room of his carved images? For they say, 'The Lord does not see us; the Lord has forsaken the land.'" —Ezekiel 8:12

We can't hide in the dark. The eyes of God never squint. When the people of Judah opted to worship created things in place of the Creator, they practiced their idolatry behind closed doors in dark quarters. As did Adam and Eve in the garden of Eden, when the people of God sinned against Him, they attempted to hide from God and continue in sin rather than expose themselves submissively in confession and repentance. We as believers ought not make our homes in darkness; rather, we are privileged to walk in the light of God (1 John 1:7). The dark idolatry Ezekiel witnessed was not unique to his day—Christians today are tempted by the pull of pornography, infidelity, greed, and gossip. Instead of indulging in the dark, it's imperative that we keep confessing our temptations and weakness, crying out to our loving God in order to remain in the warm glow of righteousness.

Ezekiel 9

The Lord said to him, "Go through the midst of the city, even through the midst of Jerusalem, and put a mark on the foreheads of the men who sigh and groan over all the abominations which are being committed in its midst." —Ezekiel 9:4

In Ezekiel's vision, written in chapter 9, God showed him the intensity of His wrath. Beginning in God's sanctuary and extending throughout Jerusalem, agents of the Lord would slay everyone, regardless of age or gender. It was a frightening scene that caused

Ezekiel to plead with God, "Are You destroying the whole remnant of Israel?" (Ezekiel 9:8). Within the city walls, though, there were people who had groaned for years over Judah's idolatry. God had heard them. Yet, in His mercy, God delayed His judgment to give idolaters time to repent. When the time of judgment arrived, the Lord honored the righteous indignation of His loyal followers—they would be protected in the day of reckoning. Do we groan today over wickedness we see? Consider the delay in God's judgment as a sign of His patient mercy, and pray that evildoers would be convicted and repent. Be confident that God hears our groans. He is slow to anger and abounding in mercy (Psalm 103:8; 2 Peter 3:9).

Ezekiel 10

Then the glory of the LORD departed from the threshold of the temple and stood over the cherubim. —*Ezekiel 10:18*

In Deuteronomy 31:17, the Lord made plain that He would remove His glory from the temple should His people stray from Him. In this vision, Ezekiel watched the Lord depart from the sanctuary built for Him. Strikingly absent from this vision are the inhabitants of Judah. The Lord's glory left the temple and *no one noticed*. Whether it was because the leaders had adapted to functioning without dependence on the Lord or because the people were so enmeshed in idolatrous activity that they became spiritually insensitive, their apathy toward God was typified by their absence from the scene. Because we have the indwelling Holy Spirit, Christians never have to fear God removing Himself from our lives. We can be encouraged to serve, worship, and live each day craving the presence and guidance of the Lord.

Ezekiel 11

"And I will give them one heart, and put a new spirit within them.
And I will take the heart of stone out of their flesh and give them
a heart of flesh, that they may walk in My statutes and keep My
ordinances and do them. Then they will be My people, and I shall be
their God."   *— Ezekiel 11:19 – 20*

Even though God disciplined His people with exile, famine, and
foreign invaders, He still promised to remain their refuge. His
plans for them did not end with dispersion but redemption. The
Lord renewed His covenant of love when He stated, "Then they
will be My people, and I shall be their God" (Ezekiel 11:20).
Part of this renewal of vows entailed a transformation of the
people — not by their own work or will but by God's volition.
Unity of heart is the first characteristic of His redeemed people.
Jesus' words to His disciples echo this standard (John 17:21 – 23).
Where God's people were previously spiritually apathetic and
selfish, God would give them a heart to pursue loyalty, righteousness, and compassion toward others. God irrevocably places His
Spirit within believers, and because of the indwelling Spirit of
God, we are a new creation (2 Corinthians 5:17). While we still
await the complete fulfillment of this passage, the Spirit empow-
ers us to love God and love our neighbor.

Ezekiel 12

"'For there will no longer be any false vision or flattering divination within the house of Israel. For I the LORD will speak, and whatever word I speak will be performed. It will no longer be delayed, for in your days, O rebellious house, I will speak the word and perform it,' declares the Lord GOD."　　　　　　　*—Ezekiel 12:24–25*

Every preacher in every pulpit isn't speaking the Word of God. In Ezekiel's day, prophets tickled the ears of the people, failing to warn them of the imminent wrath of God and refusing to exhort the people to repent of their wickedness. God holds to a high standard those who interpret His words to His people. Ezekiel had the impossible task of warning an obstinate people with God's truth in the face of isolation and ridicule and after a slew of false prophets predicted peace. Ezekiel obeyed, because exhorting the people with God's words was his most important duty. Beware of preachers who seem more concerned with how we feel about them than whether we obey the Word of God. Beware of those who compromise God's Word when it suits them. To avoid false teaching, the best strategy is to read, study, discuss, and apply the Bible daily.

Ezekiel 13

"Because you disheartened the righteous with falsehood when I did not cause him grief, but have encouraged the wicked not to turn from his wicked way and preserve his life, therefore, you women will no longer see false visions or practice divination, and I will deliver My people out of your hand. Thus you will know that I am the Lord."
—*Ezekiel 13:22–23*

Some people read horoscopes, play with Ouija boards, get their palm read, or receive tarot card readings for "harmless" fun. From tea leaves to chicken bones, people have looked to everything *but* God in order to know how to react to the present and prepare for the future. In Ezekiel's day, diviners would sell their false fortunes for a bag of barley, which Judah's population was all too eager to pay. Far too many gullible people were influenced by these twisted foretellers, who led them away from God and toward calamity. These fortune-tellers mocked the scales of justice by protecting the wicked and making vulnerable the guiltless. Believers should know that there are no shortcuts to discovering the future. Also, there is no such thing as "harmless" fortune-telling. We honor God when we place our faith and future in Him.

Ezekiel 14

"For anyone of the house of Israel or of the immigrants who stay in Israel who separates himself from Me, sets up his idols in his heart, puts right before his face the stumbling block of his iniquity, and then comes to the prophet to inquire of Me for himself, I the Lord will be brought to answer him in My own person."   —*Ezekiel 14:7*

The perpetual problem with the people of Israel was that they subscribed to a "God-plus" system: God plus the golden calf in the wilderness, God plus a king to be like other nations, God plus household idols and fortune-tellers. Ezekiel's audience wanted to consult both their idols *and* the prophets of God, but God promised an intimate audience with the person who dared try to divide His glory—a terrifying thought. The Lord said in Isaiah 42:8, "I am the LORD, that is My name; / I will not give My glory to another, / Nor My praise to graven images." We might not bow down to graven images, but we can be tempted to idolize financial security, political affiliation, or a relationship. When it comes to our relationship with God, we cannot hedge our bets by putting our faith in "God-plus."

Ezekiel 15

"Therefore, thus says the Lord GOD, 'As the wood of the vine among the trees of the forest, which I have given to the fire for fuel, so have I given up the inhabitants of Jerusalem.'" —Ezekiel 15:6

Throughout the Bible, the presence of vines and vineyards usually symbolizes fruitfulness and blessing. Jesus also referred to Himself as the vine and called His followers to abide in Him in order to be fruitful (John 15:5). In the Old Testament, Israel was symbolized as a vine (Deuteronomy 32:32; Psalm 80:8–16). In Ezekiel 15, Israel is typified as a vine by the Lord for all the worst reasons: Israel was a flimsy, useless vine, unfit even for firewood. Israel's sin rotted God's prosperity and blessing, so God promised to consume the rotten vine with fire. Only abiding in God caused Israel to thrive—and causes the believer to thrive now. Although the imagery is harsh, there is reassurance in knowing that nothing *we* do earns us God's favor—we cannot tend or grow ourselves. Remaining in Him is sufficient.

Ezekiel 16

"Then your fame went forth among the nations on account of your beauty, for it was perfect because of My splendor which I bestowed on you," declares the Lord GOD. "But you trusted in your beauty and played the harlot because of your fame, and you poured out your harlotries on every passer-by who might be willing."

—Ezekiel 16:14–15

God compared Jerusalem to an orphan left to die, whom He loved as His own wife. Ezekiel used graphic language to describe the depths of infidelity that Jerusalem had committed against the Lord. After all that God had given the city—jewelry, clothing, love, and tender care—Jerusalem betrayed Him in order to woo people who only intended to use her. Everything Jerusalem had—status, beauty, treasure, clothing—went to prostituting herself. God's disgust is palpable: *How could she?* Her flagrant sin was not unique to her time and place. We all have sinned and come short of God's glory (Romans 3:23). Our best attempt at righteousness is as vile as filthy garments (Isaiah 64:6). Each one of us is born in sin, and we are as helpless and vulnerable as newborn babies without the love and concern of our compassionate God. May we always remember the grace of God and remain faithful to His love.

Ezekiel 17

"'As I live,' declares the Lord GOD, 'Surely in the country of the king who put him on the throne, whose oath he despised and whose covenant he broke, in Babylon he shall die.'" *—Ezekiel 17:16*

Judah's vassal-king, Zedekiah, made a treaty with the Babylonian king, Nebuchadnezzar, and swore allegiance to the king—in God's name (2 Chronicles 36:11–13). Then Zedekiah broke his promise of loyalty to Babylon by aligning himself with Egypt. God was not pleased by how lightly Zedekiah took his oath, made in the name of God, even when he was dealing with the godless and corrupt empire of Babylon. It didn't matter who was on the other side of the negotiating table; as long as God's name was invoked in an oath, that oath had better be kept in order to honor the Name. God is clear on His standard for keeping promises—we must let our yeses be yes and our noes be no. We mustn't swear by heaven or earth (Matthew 5:34–37; James 5:12). We should *just keep our word*. With God, there are no "white lies" or tiers of honesty.

Ezekiel 18

"Do I have any pleasure in the death of the wicked," declares the Lord God, "rather than that he should turn from his ways and live?"
—*Ezekiel 18:23*

God the Father is perfect in His holiness, sovereign in His timing, merciful, and just. He is not a sadistic tyrant, eager to punish and slay at the first whiff of sin. It may be hard to grasp the mercy of God while reading chapter after chapter about His impending judgment, but in Ezekiel 18, God makes plain that He takes no pleasure in the death of the wicked; rather, His desire is for repentance. Although the prophecies of Ezekiel are against the people of Judah, God also makes plain that He judges each individual according to his or her actions. The weight of a sinful father won't fall on the shoulders of his daughter; likewise, the righteousness of a righteous brother is not sufficient to cover his sibling. Each person is responsible for his or her spiritual actions. In God's great and poetic grace, He does not extend this rule to Himself; He sent His sinless Son to die for our sake so that we can be made righteous through Him.

Ezekiel 19

"And fire has gone out from its branch;
It has consumed its shoots and fruit,
So that there is not in it a strong branch,
A scepter to rule."   *—Ezekiel 19:14*

In this chapter, Ezekiel recorded a song of lament on God's behalf, over the people of Israel. God personified the kingdoms of Israel and Judah by comparing their mother (who typified the kings) to a lioness and a vine. The "branch" is a Messianic theme within the Prophetic Books, referring specifically to the Davidic dynasty. The Lord had promised that the scepter would not depart from David's line (Psalm 132:11–12), but in Ezekiel 19, God's promise seemed to hang in the balance in the wake of the east wind—Babylon. Thankfully, God keeps His promises, even when His people don't. The branch was weakened, languishing in the wilderness, but still, it did not die. God would never forget Israel (Isaiah 49:15). Even in the midst of harsh chastening, God preserved His people, and the seedling of His salvation plan for humankind remained whole in order to make way for the Branch, Jesus. The Lord has not forgotten us. In dark times, we hold on to the assurance that the God of the universe preserved the Branch not only for the people of Israel but also for us through salvation by Jesus Christ.

Ezekiel 20

"But the children rebelled against Me; they did not walk in My statutes, nor were they careful to observe My ordinances, by which, if a man observes them, he will live; they profaned My sabbaths. So I resolved to pour out My wrath on them, to accomplish My anger against them in the wilderness. But I withdrew My hand and acted for the sake of My name, that it should not be profaned in the sight of the nations in whose sight I had brought them out."

—*Ezekiel 20:21–22*

The Lord is zealous for His own name. Because His name is the fullness of truth and integrity, He guarded its reputation, in part, through the way He dealt with the people of Israel. Because they were His special possession (Deuteronomy 7:6), they were supposed to keep God's ordinances and His Sabbaths. Yet generation after generation failed to even try. Ezekiel 20 recounts Israel's history of idolatry, which predated even the exodus. Time after time, God spared His people, refusing to annihilate them for besmirching His name before godless nations. Believers ought to reverence God's name at all times—it's not an epithet or a swear word or a way to casually express frustration. We ought not abuse the Lord's name—and, therefore, His graciousness—as unbelievers do. The Lord's name is sacred. Let us continually strive to be zealous for His name.

Ezekiel 21

"A ruin, a ruin, a ruin, I will make it. This also will be no more until He comes whose right it is, and I will give it to Him."

—*Ezekiel 21:27*

The word *ruin* must have echoed in Ezekiel's mind and heart as he prophesied God's words of certainty to the people. God even showed Ezekiel the routes that Babylon would take to capture Jerusalem. The recurring theme of the sword in this chapter speaks in no uncertain terms about the Lord's intention to allow violence to come to the city—even to the most privileged sanctuaries (Ezekiel 21:1)—and to the prince of Jerusalem himself (21:25–26). The Israelites were privileged to have had God as their defender in countless battles; this time, though, God was their opposition. What a frightening thought! Because of their spiritual apathy, the Israelites did not realize they were opposing God. It's so tempting to try to control and manipulate life's circumstances according to what we see, but when we take the lead away from God, we're bound to wander from God's side. When we allow God to lead, we can navigate even the unknown and depend on Him for wisdom.

Ezekiel 22

"The people of the land have practiced oppression and committed robbery, and they have wronged the poor and needy and have oppressed the sojourner without justice. I searched for a man among them who would build up the wall and stand in the gap before Me for the land, so that I would not destroy it; but I found no one."

—*Ezekiel 22:29–30*

Have you ever watched TV shows with hidden cameras and actors in disguise? They place unwitting people into orchestrated scenarios of conflict . . . just to see what, if anything, they do to resolve problems, defend the defenseless, or shame the wrong-doer. Some people emerged as heroes; they did the brave thing because it was the right thing to do. Many more people, though, stood idly by and watched others receive unjust treatment. When interviewed about their apathy, they said they "didn't want to get involved." In God's eyes, apathy is a form of wickedness. Judah's leaders constantly ripped apart the most vulnerable. Would any of God's people come to the defense of the most vulner-able — the widow, orphan, and foreigner? No one stood in the gap. Thank God we live on this side of Jesus' death and resurrec-tion! Jesus stood in the gap for us all, and because He did, we are not destroyed. Let us live like Him and stand in the gap for the needy and vulnerable in our communities, nation, and world.

Ezekiel 23

"Therefore, thus says the Lord GOD, 'Because you have forgotten Me and cast Me behind your back, bear now the punishment of your lewdness and your harlotries.'" —Ezekiel 23:35

This chapter contains some of the roughest language and imagery in the entire Bible. Why? Because the Lord wanted to communicate in the strongest terms possible the depth of Judah's (Oholibah) and Israel's (Oholah) idolatry—the intimate, vile, reprehensible betrayal committed against Him. Their faith, their love, their energy, their resources were all given to anyone but the God who delivered and prospered them. They trusted in Assyria and Babylon and Egypt to save them from political problems—after God had led them to countless military victories; after He had provided food, land, treasure, and children; and after He had given them the Law to keep them safe and cause them to shine like a beacon to glorify God. God's anger toward this betrayal was unquenchable; there was no repentance or return imagery in this prophecy. The truth is, we all stand guilty of playing the harlot against God (Isaiah 53:6), which is why we need a Savior—the ultimate Deliverer—who both saved us and stood in our place to receive God's wrath. Let us never forget the depth of our sin and the vastness of God's compassion and grace. May these truths spur us on to faithfulness.

Ezekiel 24

So I spoke to the people in the morning, and in the evening my wife died. And in the morning I did as I was commanded. —Ezekiel 24:18

Our lives are not our own. They're not. We are vessels of God, made to glorify Him, and our lives are best lived when yielded to Him. But a yielded life is not an easy life. God prompted the death of Ezekiel's wife and ordered him not to mourn for her (Ezekiel 24:16–17) as a sign to the people that the sanctuary they delighted in was about to be profaned. The people had taken for granted their covenant relationship with the Lord, and the temple had become a symbol of their pride rather than their devotion. God promised to strip them of that pride, take their children, and give them no opportunity to mourn their losses because they would be immediately snatched into captivity. Wrapped up in all the symbolism, though, was Ezekiel's faithfulness to God and to delivering His message, even when it cost him his dear wife. Are we so yielded to God that He can count on our faithful living, no matter what?

Ezekiel 25

"I will execute great vengeance on them with wrathful rebukes;
and they will know that I am the Lord when I lay My vengeance
on them."   —*Ezekiel 25:17*

Ezekiel's prophecies were mainly focused on Judah, but in this chapter, the cities of Ammon, Moab, and Philistia received warnings from God in response to their treachery against Judah. Even though the Lord was about to discipline Judah, Jerusalem was still His treasured possession. He promised to take vengeance on those who taunted and victimized Judah. The Lord had made known that vengeance was His to repay (Deuteronomy 32:35). In Deuteronomy, God's vengeance on His people's behalf was also tied to their idolatry. He knew the day of His vengeance would come *after* He was betrayed, after He chastened His people, and after they were so weak and powerless that only He could save them. But God *never* abandons His own, even when they reject or betray Him. He is ever faithful. We may fail and fall, but we cannot be plucked out of the ever-loving hand of God (John 10:28–29), and He promises to defend us and to right the wrongs done to us (Revelation 19:11–21).

Ezekiel 26

For thus says the Lord God, "Behold, I will bring upon Tyre from the
north Nebuchadnezzar king of Babylon, king of kings, with horses,
chariots, cavalry and a great army."   —*Ezekiel 26:7*

If God says He will do something, trust that He will. In chapter 26, Ezekiel foretold that Nebuchadnezzar, king of Babylon, would invade Jerusalem. After that, according to Ezekiel's prophecy, many nations would rise up against Tyre. The city would be flattened, and ultimately it would cease to exist. In the sixth century BC, King Nebuchadnezzar laid siege to Tyre until the city was subdued (Ezekiel 26:7). Next, Alexander the Great built a land bridge to conquer Tyre's remaining island fortress. His army slaughtered the inhabitants and reduced the island to rubble. Much later, during the Crusades, the Muslims invaded Tyre with no resistance, slaughtered its inhabitants, and tore down all of its structures. Since then, Tyre has not been rebuilt but is instead a fishing pit stop to cast and spread nets (26:14). This is one small example of God's faithfulness to complete His promises. Trust Him — He keeps His word.

Ezekiel 27

"When your wares went out from the seas,
You satisfied many peoples;
With the abundance of your wealth and your merchandise
You enriched the kings of earth.
Now that you are broken by the seas
In the depths of the waters,
Your merchandise and all your company
Have fallen in the midst of you."   —*Ezekiel 27:33–34*

The Lord sang a lament for Tyre in chapter 27. In what began as a lovely eulogy, He described the beauty, strength, power, and influence of the region, especially focusing on its maritime prowess. But in 27:27, the seas on which Tyre so heavily depended for its livelihood became the vehicle of the country's demise. The Lord is the Master of the seas and can better control the waters than even the celebrated sailors of Tyre. Tyre thought of itself as the master of the sea because of its pride. Its destruction would be poetic justice and a sign to the surrounding countries who admired it that God alone is sovereign over all the earth. A country may seem to prosper outside the will of God, but *everything*, even a corrupt administration's success, yields to the will of God (Proverbs 21:1). We must remember that no country is outside of God's control, no matter the depths of its power.

Ezekiel 28

"'Will you still say, "I am a god,"
In the presence of your slayer,
Though you are a man and not God,
In the hands of those who wound you?
You will die the death of the uncircumcised
By the hand of strangers,
For I have spoken!' declares the Lord GOD!"   *—Ezekiel 28:9–10*

Ezekiel 28 is one of the most difficult passages for scholars to parse. It raises the question: is the king of Tyre a type of Adam? Or is he a false god? Or is he Satan? Most likely, Satan is being described in 28:11–19—when the prophecy switched from addressing the "leader" of Tyre to the "king" of Tyre. Satan was in Eden, created as more than a man, and fell short of perfection because of his prideful pursuit to be a god. Whoever is in view is supremely guilty of the sin of hubris. Tyre's leader made the mistake of referring to himself as a god. Not only was the king guilty of pride, which put him in direct opposition to God, but he also practiced the most narcissistic idolatry possible by deifying himself. The king of Tyre put a target on his own head. In today's "selfie" world, crammed with exercise fads, enhancement drugs, surgeries, cosmetics, and diets, we can easily fall prey to narcissistic idolatry. Our society worships itself. Humility and dependence on God is the antidote to the poison of self-centeredness.

Ezekiel 29

"And it will never again be the confidence of the house of Israel, bringing to mind the iniquity of their having turned to Egypt. Then they will know that I am the Lord GOD."
—*Ezekiel 29:16*

In Egyptian mythology, pharaohs controlled the Nile. In Ezekiel's prophecy, the pharaoh was not lord over the Nile; he was a mere fish, easily baited and caught by sovereign God (Ezekiel 29:4). God planned to attack the waterways of Egypt and make them desolate for forty years (29:11–12). Israel had looked to Egypt — rather than Yahweh — as a great power and potential military ally. Once the Lord used foreign invaders to neutralize Egypt, the people of Israel would never again look to it as their possible source of salvation. God is jealous for His own name's sake (Exodus 34:14). He doesn't tolerate being used as a supplementary or symbolic deity. He is the Lord, and there is no other — no other safety net, no other means of security, no other more important relationship, no other person who should be revered before Him.

Ezekiel 30

"For I will strengthen the arms of the king of Babylon and put My sword in his hand; and I will break the arms of Pharaoh, so that he will groan before him with the groanings of a wounded man."
—*Ezekiel 30:24*

Isn't it infuriating when a reckless driver gets ahead? For that guy, all the lights are green, all the state troopers are occupied, and all the drivers acquiesce. Why does that guy get to get ahead while we follow the rules and catch all the red lights? Why would God strengthen the arm of a terrible nation like Babylon when

He could have well used His own people — at least in name — to mete out justice? The short and maybe even unsatisfying answer is it's not our business. It can't be: we are finite, self-interested, and sinful. In Ezekiel, Babylon was a tool in the hand of a justice-wielding God — but He had devastating plans for Babylon too. We don't know the plans He has for the reckless driver; we need to have faith that though we're sitting at the red lights of life, God's sovereignty still stands.

Ezekiel 31

"Behold, Assyria was a cedar in Lebanon
With beautiful branches and forest shade,
And very high,
And its top was among the clouds."   *— Ezekiel 31:3*

Ezekiel employed the metaphor of a tree — the cedar of Lebanon — to describe Assyria. Cedars of Lebanon grew as tall as 120 feet, and were known for their durability and fragrance. They were used in the construction of King David's palace (2 Samuel 5:11) and King Solomon's temple (1 Kings 6:9). These particular cedars were strong, tall, flawless trees with no known predators — trees that, without an act of God, would flourish forever. Egypt thought of itself as Assyria's equal (Ezekiel 31:2–3). But like Egypt, Assyria took pride in itself and would fall before foreign invaders, specifically Babylon. We can occupy ourselves with comparisons and efforts to "keep up with the Joneses," but when we do, we're using the wrong measuring stick. The Lord alone commends (2 Corinthians 10:17–18).

Ezekiel 32

"And when I extinguish you,
I will cover the heavens and darken their stars;
I will cover the sun with a cloud
And the moon will not give its light.
All the shining lights in the heavens
I will darken over you
And will set darkness on your land,"
Declares the Lord God.   *— Ezekiel 32:7 – 8*

Egyptians worshiped a pantheon of gods and goddesses and considered their pharaoh a god. One of the most venerated Egyptian deities was Ra, the sun god. Egyptian monarchs considered themselves sons of Ra because of the power they claimed he possessed. Ezekiel's forecast of Egypt's doom confronted their belief system: Egypt may have been like a "lion" to the nations (Ezekiel 32:2) — a royal symbol evident in the sphinxes that adorned the Egyptian kingdom — but would be nothing more than a sea creature to be caught in God's net. It would be *dark* when they were extinguished — so they were sure to know that their sun god, Ra, was not the one, true God. Ezekiel's prophecy simultaneously recalled the plagues before the exodus, the dark imagery of the eschatological last days, and the unequivocal assertion that God alone is God. Take comfort knowing that God confronts religious falsehood with calculated power. God is the best and most efficient defender of His own name.

Ezekiel 33

"Say to them, 'As I live!' declares the Lord GOD, 'I take no pleasure in the death of the wicked, but rather that the wicked turn from his way and live. Turn back, turn back from your evil ways! Why then will you die, O house of Israel?'" —*Ezekiel 33:11*

The people of Israel were given a choice: rebel or repent. Receive God's mercy and forgiveness or reject it in order to pursue self-ish desires. Israel chose rebellion and rejection and faced the harsh consequences of their sin. Was God thrilled to afflict the people of Israel? Was He a sadistic disciplinarian, just waiting for His people to fail so He could let them have it? No. God was eager to bless them, but He also kept His word, like the good Father He is. God's desire was to bring life and restora-tion to His people; therefore, He couldn't allow His people to stray without warning and discipline. When we reject God and rebel, we are choosing death instead of the abundant life God has for us. This chapter records the exiles' discovery that Jerusalem had been taken (Ezekiel 33:21). What if the people of Israel had acted upon Ezekiel's warnings instead of being entertained yet unmoved (33:32)?

Ezekiel 34

"Then I will set over them one shepherd, My servant David, and he will feed them; he will feed them himself and be their shepherd." —*Ezekiel 34:23*

Good leaders inspire, protect, challenge, and serve. The lead-ership of both Israel and Judah had drawn the anger of God because they disregarded holiness and acted more like preda-tors than protectors of God's flock. These leaders filled their bellies and clothed themselves with sacrifices set apart for God (Ezekiel 34:3), neglected the sick and vulnerable (34:4), and allowed the flock to wander away spiritually (34:5). God stepped in to protect His people from predatory leadership and offered hope through the Good Shepherd. In this Messianic passage, Ezekiel prophesied of the descendant of David who would protect His sheep. No wonder Matthew wrote of Jesus: "Seeing the people, He felt compassion for them, because they were distressed and dispirited like sheep without a shepherd" (Matthew 9:36). Remember the marks of a good shepherd: one who strengthens the weak, cares for the sick, seeks those who stray, and searches for the lost.

Ezekiel 35

"As you rejoiced over the inheritance of the house of Israel because it was desolate, so I will do to you. You will be a desolation, O Mount Seir, and all Edom, all of it. Then they will know that I am the LORD."
— Ezekiel 35:15

Edom — the region of Jacob's (or Israel's) brother, Esau — was first in line as an enemy to Israel. When Israel had yet to possess the Promised Land, thirsty and weary from wilderness living, they asked to pass through the land of Edom. The citizens of Edom violently refused Israel's passage (Numbers 20:18, 20), chasing away people who were essentially the relatives of Edom's citizens. God had not forgotten the maltreatment of His people, and He called out Edom for its ungodly treatment of Israel. At the root of Edom's disdain was a disregard for the Lord (Ezekiel 35:13). A wrong view of God precedes the mistreatment of people. Because people are made in the image of God, the mercy, compassion, hatred, or indifference we show each other demonstrates our level of regard for the Lord who created us. God's people should make no room for jealousy, malice, slander, or hatred in their interactions with others (Ephesians 4:31–32).

Ezekiel 36

"I will vindicate the holiness of My great name which has been profaned among the nations, which you have profaned in their midst. Then the nations will know that I am the LORD," declares the Lord GOD, "when I prove Myself holy among you in their sight."

—*Ezekiel 36:23*

Ezekiel's prophecies turned a *major* corner in this chapter! Prior to this chapter, oracle after oracle predicted imminent woe, but now God's discipline of Israel was ending. God spoke of restoration, beginning with the mountains (Ezekiel 36:8). It might sound bizarre—God reassuring the ground—but the whole creation groans because of the weight of sin (Romans 8:21–22), and all of creation will be redeemed, both in the millennium and the new heaven and earth. As God restores the land, He will restore the people of Israel (Ezekiel 36:25–29), cleanse them, remove their stony hearts, and give them a heart for the Lord and His Spirit. Just as the mountains are helpless in their state, the people of Israel could not return to God without His direct intervention. For His name's sake, Israel would be Spirit-empowered to regard Him as holy. Because Christians have the Holy Spirit, we, too, can declare the holiness of God by how well we treat others and even how we steward the resources God gives us.

Ezekiel 37

He said to me, "Son of man, can these bones live?" And I answered,
"O Lord GOD, You know." —*Ezekiel 37:3*

The valley of dry bones is one of the most well-known images in
the Old Testament. The long-dead seem hopeless in their state.
It's over for them, isn't it? This is the question that God asked
Ezekiel—who couldn't have answered any better than "Lord,
You know" . . . especially after he'd received oracle after oracle of
death and desolation concerning Israel. Just as at one time Adam
lie lifeless as formed dirt (Genesis 2:7), the valley of bones lie
desolate and waiting for the breath and the will of God to cause
them to live. God promises life, land, restoration, unity, and
prosperity under One King for Israel. The promises may have
seemed as dead as the dry-bones valley to the people of Jesus'
day—but, oh, how they must have quaked with hope the day
Jesus brought Lazarus back from the grave (John 11:43–45). In
Jesus' yet future thousand-year reign, Ezekiel's vision of restoration and peace will be fully realized for Israel. And we believers
can take comfort that God's resurrection power will, at any
moment, change our mortal bodies to be like Jesus' resurrected
body. For those of us who have died, God will pull us from our
graves, breathe life into our everlasting bodies, and resurrect us
to enjoy eternal life with Him (1 Thessalonians 4:13–17).

Ezekiel 38

"And you will come up against My people Israel like a cloud to cover
the land. It shall come about in the last days that I will bring you
against My land, so that the nations may know Me when I am sanc-
tified through you before their eyes, O Gog." —*Ezekiel 38:16*

In chapter 37, Ezekiel prophesied about the restoration of Israel that will occur with the advent of Jesus' millennial rule. This chapter contrasts the light and freedom of the millennium with the evil that desires to oppose God, personified through Gog. Magog, with its cities of Tubal and Rosh—obscure names to our ears—was a region that may have existed historically in Lydia, but it typifies the kingdoms assembled against God in the end times. After the millennium (Revelation 20:7–9), Gog will come against Israel with a great army (Ezekiel 38:9). Though the timeline and names may be confusing or hard to fathom, know this: Gog and his armies, deceived by Satan, attempt to battle God, but God, in His holy anger, rains down fire and pestilence (38:22). Death and evil are utterly conquered. God and we, His people, live happily ever after. God wins.

Ezekiel 39

*Therefore thus says the Lord G*OD*, "Now I will restore the fortunes of Jacob and have mercy on the whole house of Israel; and I will be jealous for My holy name."*

—Ezekiel 39:25

If Ezekiel 38 is a wide-angle focus of the battle between God and the armies of the world led by Gog, Ezekiel 39 is a telephoto focus on *how* and *why* God wins the battle. Ezekiel prophesied concerning God's strategy in trouncing the foes of His people and magnifying Himself. God is zealous for His people; the defeat of their enemies will be so extensive that God will dedicate *seven months* to find and bury their remains (Ezekiel 39:12). This sound defeat will accomplish two ends: to secure Israel in its own land, unafraid (39:26) and to sanctify the name of God among the nations (39:27). As Christians, how does this apply to us? We can be confident in the perfect justice of God and His ability to defend His name and His people in His timing.

Ezekiel 40

The man said to me, "Son of man, see with your eyes, hear with your ears, and give attention to all that I am going to show you; for you have been brought here in order to show it to you. Declare to the house of Israel all that you see."

—*Ezekiel 40:4*

Fourteen years after Jerusalem was besieged (Ezekiel 40:1), God granted Ezekiel the vision (and incredible memory for detail) of His rebuilt temple. With care and specificity, the Lord imparted to Ezekiel His sanctuary design plans. Not just visions of a worship structure, the sanctuary visions were also a reassurance of the Lord's return. In contrast to chapters 8–11, when God's glory left the temple and the city, in this chapter, the Lord described the structures in the outer courts (which formerly were cracked and covered with carvings of abominations described in 8:7–10). Singers and priests who attend God's altar are to dwell there—no more idolatry, just true worship. God crafted meticulous plans for His house of worship, communicated to His people that He would fulfill His promises of restoration, and encouraged the hearts of the people of Israel that they would not always live in exile. The temple described here has yet to be built, but the specificity in detail serves as assurance to believers. God's promises are faithful to be completed to His exact specifications.

Ezekiel 41

He measured its length, twenty cubits, and the width, twenty cubits, before the nave; and he said to me, "This is the most holy place."
—*Ezekiel 41:4*

When taking a tour of Buckingham Palace or the White House, how close to the monarch's or president's private offices can a person get? Royals, presidents, celebrities . . . all have protocols in place to keep out unauthorized people and allow in only designated people. The temple—God's holy place—was a space infinitely more significant and separate. Only the High Priest would be allowed into the inner sanctuary; most priests solely dedicated to the service of God would *never* enter into this space. Yet in this chapter, Ezekiel described the dimensions of the inner and outer sanctuary, the walls, and the platform of the temple because he was granted access by the Lord Himself. Believers now have an all-access pass to the throne of grace (Hebrews 4:16) because Jesus Himself is our High Priest. He makes us holy.

Ezekiel 42

He measured it on the four sides; it had a wall all around, the length five hundred and the width five hundred, to divide between the holy and the profane.
—*Ezekiel 42:20*

God is holy. Because He is holy, He requires those who serve Him to be holy. The temple in Ezekiel's vision was constructed to ensure separation between the holy places and the profane ones. Ezekiel described the designated places for priests to eat and change in to and out of their set-apart vestments. They even had a designated entryway. The priests were perpetually prone to defilement; God required them to set themselves apart to decrease their chances of becoming unclean (Haggai 2:11–14). One of the amazing distinctions of Jesus from the rest of humanity is His impregnable holiness. Where others would be made unclean by the presence of sickness, defilement, or sin, Jesus could face it all . . . and transform it, revive it, restore it. His holiness, unlike a priest's, is not a function of place or dress or subject to defilement at any given time. Holiness is who He *is*. Jesus is the incredible bridge between sin-sick humanity and the throne of holy God. As Christ-followers, we can emulate Jesus through our compassion and care for our society's "untouchables."

Ezekiel 43

"If they are ashamed of all that they have done, make known to them the design of the house, its structure, its exits, its entrances, all its designs, all its statutes, and all its laws. And write it in their sight, so that they may observe its whole design and all its statutes and do them." —*Ezekiel 43:11*

In Ezekiel 11:23, the Lord's glory left the temple, and the people, even with Ezekiel's oracles, did not notice because their abominations were so great. In this chapter, Ezekiel envisioned the Lord's glory returning to the temple (Ezekiel 43:2). God would again commune with His people, but only *after* they experienced genuine remorse over their sin (43:11). How majestic and powerful the temple plans must be that they alone could be enough to prick the people's hearts to repentance. Perhaps the plans would serve as a reminder of the temple that they had lost because of their rebellion. In the millennium, when Christ will be physically present with His people, God will once again accept temple sacrifices (43:27) — likely to serve as a memorial for Christ's sacrifice. Next time we participate in communion, we can ponder these things.

Ezekiel 44

"It shall be that when they enter at the gates of the inner court, they shall be clothed with linen garments; and wool shall not be on them while they are ministering in the gates of the inner court and in the house."
—*Ezekiel 44:17*

Why do men and women who serve in uniform adhere to regulations concerning their dress—the color and knit of their clothing? The uniform serves double duty as a way to identify the person's specialty or occupation while also allowing him or her some anonymity. Uniforms are not a vehicle of self-expression; rather, to those who view them, the uniform gives honor to the organization it represents. God outlined the protocol and hierarchy of the priests whom He chose to serve before Him and the people within the new temple. God's detail was necessary because the priests represented the holy God they served. All aspects of the priests—from their hair, to their linen turbans and vestments, to the wives they chose, even to their lack of land rights—were to remind people of the holiness of God. Christians represent the Lord in all we are (Romans 12:1), and our uniform—that which unites us to God and to other Christians—is love (John 17:22–23; Romans 13:8–10).

Ezekiel 45

"You shall have just balances, a just ephah and a just bath."
—*Ezekiel 45:10*

We all likely use scales to weigh produce at the grocery store. The butcher uses a scale to measure and charge customers for beef, chicken, and fish. More than two thousand years have passed since Ezekiel's prophecies, but most of society still use scales in their transactions. Even in the time of Israel's restoration, Ezekiel's prophecy was a reminder to the leadership—the "princes" of Ezekiel 45:9—to use "just balances"—to charge people only what they owed instead of manipulating scales to garner a larger profit or encroach on other people's land in order to expand their property. Corrupt scales led Israel into judgment (Ezekiel 22:12) and have no place in the millennial kingdom. God is not anti-commerce, but He is opposed to deceit, exploitation of the less fortunate, and dishonest gain. Those in the corporate world best represent God when their creativity, professional relationships, and business practices reflect integrity and accuracy.

Ezekiel 46

"And you shall provide a lamb a year old without blemish for a burnt offering to the LORD daily; morning by morning you shall provide it."
—*Ezekiel 46:13*

Ezekiel 46 details the series of sacrifices that will take place daily in the millennial temple—during the future thousand-year earthly reign of Christ. Scholars debate whether the sacrifices themselves will serve as a method of atonement or whether they will serve as a memorial to Jesus' sacrificial work during His first coming. It seems that these sacrifices will indeed be a flesh-and-blood, tactile memorial of the depth of love that God demonstrated through Jesus Christ—hearing the bleating of a year-old lamb being offered up *every single day* will doubtless remind the people of the Lamb of God—and also will be a reminder of every mortal's need for atonement. Like manna that came down in the wilderness morning by morning (Exodus 16:13–15), the bleating lamb will symbolize God's mercy and forgiveness, fresh for that day. Even now, believers can remember and cultivate gratitude for new mercies, morning by morning.

Ezekiel 47

"By the river on its bank, on one side and on the other, will grow all kinds of trees for food. Their leaves will not wither and their fruit will not fail. They will bear every month because their water flows from the sanctuary, and their fruit will be for food and their leaves for healing." —*Ezekiel 47:12*

Earlier in the book of Ezekiel, God asked Ezekiel to prophesy to the mountains of Israel, telling them that they will no longer be known as a "devourer of men" (Ezekiel 36:13) and will no longer be defiled by the abominations of His rebellious people. In fact, the land will be treated better than at the first (36:11). In chapter 47, the Lord detailed the nourishing, healing, and fruitfulness of the land. There will be streams of water flowing from the sanctuary, because the land, as the people, will not thirst anymore (Revelation 21:6, 22:1–2). This is a time when humankind and nature will be in peaceful subjection to the King, a time when the earth will flourish in an idyllic state that surpasses even the garden of Eden. It's hard to imagine in our world's current state what glorious redemption awaits every aspect of existence, but redemption is coming! We must continue to encourage one another with these words until the time of fulfillment comes.

Ezekiel 48

"The city shall be 18,000 cubits round about; and the name of the city from that day shall be, 'The Lord is there.'" —*Ezekiel 48:35*

The book of Ezekiel begins in a foreign land with the people of Israel sitting by a river in Babylon, but it ends in the Promised Land with the tribes of Israel reunited—each with an allotment of land parceled out personally by God. What hopeful words after so many years and oracles of woe! God is faithful to keep His promises to Israel, and because of Israel, all the nations are indeed blessed. Believers get to witness the fulfillment of Israel's destiny in the yet future millennium and walk the streets of the New Jerusalem after that (Revelation 21:9–10). The best and brightest blessing will be fellowship with God. "The LORD is there" (Ezekiel 48:35) characterizes the future city because, in contrast to the beginning of the book of Ezekiel, God's presence will pervade every part of life, every inhabitant will know Him, the land will be blessed, and the nations will bow down to the One True King. The future city will be named "the Lord is there," but our present Savior is named "God with us." We can rejoice that Jesus is our present help, our Advocate, and our High Priest — right now.

Daniel

Daniel 1

But Daniel made up his mind that he would not defile himself with the king's choice food or with the wine which he drank; so he sought permission from the commander of the officials that he might not defile himself. —*Daniel 1:8*

Chosen as one of the best and brightest of all the Jews, Daniel entered King Nebuchadnezzar's leadership training academy. Daniel and his fellow elite Hebrews were offered the king's food, the best wine, and the potential to serve as high-ranking officials in Babylon. Because of his social position, pride could have swelled in Daniel's heart, crowding out God, but it didn't. While both honor and temptations rained down on Daniel, he kept his heart pure by practicing the same spiritual disciplines he had practiced throughout his life: prayer and fasting. Daniel refused to eat the king's food which probably had been first offered to false gods. But Daniel didn't wait until temptation was right before him to decide whether or not to succumb to it. Daniel chose beforehand not to defile himself or disobey God while in service to the king. For Christians, spiritual discipline must be a way of life. Like Daniel, we must make up our minds to prepare us for temptations before they strike.

Daniel 2

"However, there is a God in heaven who reveals mysteries, and He has made known to King Nebuchadnezzar what will take place in the latter days. This was your dream and the visions in your mind while on your bed."   —*Daniel 2:28*

Daniel gave credit where credit was due. He praised God as the discerner of dreams. Daniel could have easily taken the credit for interpreting King Nebuchadnezzar's dream, and no one would have known except God. Daniel could have made his reputation as the smartest, most gifted prophet in Babylon. But because Daniel performed for an audience of One, he only cared what God thought about him. And Daniel wanted the king to know God's power and that He alone deserved worship. Do we take credit for the blessings, abilities, and open doors God has given us? Do we take credit because we're too embarrassed to mention God's work in our lives? Or do we really believe that God is responsible for all the good things that happen to us? All good things come from God (James 1:17). When He blesses us, He wants others to know so they can worship Him too.

Daniel 3

"But even if He does not, let it be known to you, O king, that we are not going to serve your gods or worship the golden image that you have set up."   —*Daniel 3:18*

Shadrach, Meshach, and Abednego refused to worship King Nebuchadnezzar's idol. Ready to die for their faith, these men entrusted themselves to God's sovereignty *even though* He allowed them to be thrown in the furnace. Miraculously,

God delivered these men from the fire, but He didn't have to. Shadrach, Meshach, and Abednego vowed to worship Him in spite of their impending martyrdom. How often do we promise our devotion and sacrifice *only if* God will do something for us first? Shouldn't it be the other way around — worship God, devote ourselves to Him, and sacrifice our lives to Him *before* He blesses us or gives us what we want? Or better, shouldn't we conduct our lives as living sacrifices even if God doesn't give us what we want — even if He allows pain and trials? We should continually examine whether our faith is based on what God does for us or on His holy and sovereign character.

Daniel 4

"I saw a dream and it made me fearful; and these fantasies as I lay on my bed and the visions in my mind kept alarming me."

—*Daniel 4:5*

Nebuchadnezzar awoke drenched. His heart pounded. Fear flooded his mind as he tried to comprehend the meaning of his nightmare. The king called Daniel to explain what the massive tree symbolized and why an angel chopped it down. As Daniel interpreted, the king had a gnawing sense that the dream was about him. Nebuchadnezzar remembered that God had given him several chances to acknowledge Yahweh as the true King. Instead, Nebuchadnezzar took credit for his great empire and was enthralled with his own dominion. The time had come, therefore, for the Lord to humble the Babylonian king and to remind him who was really in charge. God made Nebuchadnezzar live as a beast for seven years until he knelt before the true, sovereign King. Throughout our lives, God gives us opportunities to acknowledge His sovereignty and to trust Him. When we reject Him, He allows the consequences to get our attention and produce humility within us.

Daniel 5

"'TEKEL'—you have been weighed on the scales and found deficient."
                                                                    —Daniel 5:27

When a man's hand appeared out of thin air and wrote on the wall a message for King Belshazzar, the color drained from the king's face. When a Hebrew captive interpreted the foreign words on the plaster wall, the king trembled. And when the writing on the wall came true that very night when Darius the Mede took over the throne, King Belshazzar faced death for his pride. So what did those words mean that caused the Babylonian king so much fear and eventually death? For too long King Belshazzar had mocked the Lord and refused to acknowledge His supremacy. So God *weighed* and *examined* King Belshazzar's heart and judged him for taking lightly the sovereignty and justice of the Lord. Do we, as Christ followers, take lightly God's sovereign will, pretending that we hold the reins in our lives? As God's children, Christians face the Lord's scrutiny and, if necessary, His discipline.

Daniel 6

Then the king went off to his palace and spent the night fasting, and no entertainment was brought before him; and his sleep fled from him. —*Daniel 6:18*

On the night that Daniel spent in the cave with several hungry lions, King Darius lost his appetite. Darius found no satisfaction in the pastimes that usually brought him pleasure. And until he could find out the fate of his friend, Daniel, the king lay awake with insomnia. At the thought of losing Daniel, his close advisor and trusted confidant, King Darius sank into the depths of depression. Even though King Darius was the pagan king of the Medo-Persian Empire and Daniel was a Hebrew captive who worshiped Yahweh, these two men cared for each other. Daniel had built a relationship with the pagan king by faithfully serving him. Do we as believers look for ways to build friendships with nonbelievers? Do we have any close relationships with nonbelievers marked by deep concern for one another? Do any non-Christians know us well enough to see God working in our lives?

Daniel 7

"I kept looking
Until thrones were set up,
And the Ancient of Days took His seat;
His vesture was like white snow
And the hair of His head like pure wool.
His throne was ablaze with flames,
Its wheels were a burning fire." —*Daniel 7:9*

As if watching four myth-like animals trounce around the earth wasn't strange enough (Daniel 7:3 – 8), Daniel then watched as

God Himself, dressed in gleaming white, sat on His majestic throne. The throne of God had wheels of flaming fire, showing that the Ancient of Days could execute His sovereign will anywhere and everywhere throughout the entire universe. From the base of God's throne flowed a river of fire that divided the crowds of thousands upon thousands of servants and worshipers. The eternal Ancient of Days ruled as judge of the whole world. At this grand vision, Daniel could do nothing but stand in awe and worship the eternal, sovereign Lord. Are we in awe of the Lord; are we overwhelmed by His piercing holiness and His absolute sovereignty? Or are we so familiar with God that we have lost the wonder that should inspire our worship? Let's bow with Daniel before the awesome Ancient of Days.

Daniel 8

And I heard the voice of a man between the banks of Ulai, and he called out and said, "Gabriel, give this man an understanding of the vision." —Daniel 8:16

As he served the king in Susa, Daniel received a vision from God. But this vision wasn't of a lofty, heavenly scene. Rather, Daniel's strange vision featured a super-sized ram and a huge goat with extra horns. As Daniel watched the goat fly across the earth and destroy the ram, the angel Gabriel came and stood before him. God commanded Gabriel to help Daniel understand the meaning of the vision. Gabriel, whose name points to God's strength, gave Daniel wisdom and strength to understand God's prophecy. Even though we won't receive a Daniel-like revelation from the Lord and a personal visit from an angel to give us an explanation, God does send His angels to assist and encourage believers today. "Are they not all ministering spirits, sent out to render service for the sake of those who will inherit salvation?" (Hebrews 1:14).

Daniel 9

In the first year of his reign, I, Daniel, observed in the books the number of the years which was revealed as the word of the LORD to Jeremiah the prophet for the completion of the desolations of Jerusalem, namely, seventy years. —Daniel 9:2

Daniel had been reading Jeremiah's scroll containing God's promise to deliver His people after seventy years of captivity and to judge Babylon (Jeremiah 25:11–12). Daniel had also been watching the calendar. He did the math. Because God's people had lived in Babylon as captives for almost seventy years, Daniel started praying that God would forgive His people for their disobedience and deliver them just as He had promised Jeremiah. So why did Daniel pray for God to act when He had already said that He would? Daniel viewed prayer not as a lucky charm to get God to do what he wanted but as a way to align Daniel's heart, thoughts, and plans with God's. In fact, that's just how Jesus taught us to pray: "Father . . . *your* will be done" (Matthew 6:10, emphasis added). Do we pray in order to align ourselves with God's plans for us, or do we pray to ask Him to bless *our* plans?

Daniel 10

"But the prince of the kingdom of Persia was withstanding me for twenty-one days; then behold, Michael, one of the chief princes, came to help me, for I had been left there with the kings of Persia."
—*Daniel 10:13*

Daniel's mind raced as he tried to comprehend the visions God had given him. Overwhelmed, Daniel fell to his knees and begged for heavenly wisdom. As a result of Daniel's humble prayers, God sent an angel to give Daniel wisdom. But in a countermove, Satan unleashed one of his minions to block God's answer to Daniel's prayers. Then for three weeks, God's angel fought Satan's demon in a supernatural battle that would put the best action movies to shame. It wasn't until the archangel Michael came to help defeat the demon that God's answer to Daniel's prayers could reach him. Sometimes, when it seems like God doesn't hear our prayers, we must stop and remember that we live in the midst of a spiritual battle between God's heavenly armies and Satan's demonic soldiers. Prayer, then, is our greatest weapon (Ephesians 6:18). When we just want to give up, let's remember that Christ has already won the battle.

Daniel 11

"In the first year of Darius the Mede, I arose to be an encouragement and a protection for him."   —*Daniel 11:1*

When Darius (also known as Cyrus in Daniel 10:1) became the king of the Medo-Persian Empire, God had a plan for him. God intended to use Darius to send His people back to their land and initiate the temple rebuilding project in Jerusalem (2 Chronicles 36:22–23). Darius realized that God had given him power and a role to play in His unfolding plan. Satan also recognized Darius as God's chosen vessel to set free the captive Jews and to reestablish true worship in Jerusalem. While Satan sent his demons to try to thwart God's plan, God sent His angels Gabriel and Michael to fortify Darius (Daniel 10:20–11:1). Satan knew that when the Jews were back in their land, the world would be one step closer to Messiah's arrival. Satan hates Christians and focuses his efforts on snuffing out the name of Christ. Christians should not fear Satan, but we should be aware of his schemes.

Daniel 12

"But as for you, Daniel, conceal these words and seal up the book until the end of time; many will go back and forth, and knowledge will increase." —Daniel 12:4

An increase in knowledge doesn't automatically lead to an increase in wisdom. Daniel's angelic messenger told him to seal up the visions that God had given him. With each succeeding kingdom that God planned to raise up, intelligence would grow, technological innovations would improve life, and medical advances would extend life. But knowledge of the Lord wouldn't necessarily increase. If the smartest people in the world don't know and fear the Lord, they shouldn't call themselves wise (Psalm 14:1). What do we pursue above all else: more knowledge or more wisdom? Knowledge does have value, and we have a responsibility to gain knowledge that will help us excel in our careers, our parenting, our ministry, and other valid pursuits. But while knowledge has only a limited scope, godly wisdom has profit for *all* of our endeavors. So how do we acquire wisdom? Ask God for it (James 1:5).

Hosea

Hosea 1

Yet the number of the sons of Israel
Will be like the sand of the sea,
Which cannot be measured or numbered;
And in the place
Where it is said to them,
"You are not My people,"
It will be said to them,
"You are the sons of the living God."   —*Hosea 1:10*

Hosea proposed to Gomer, and she said yes. Their marriage started well, but it went south after they had kids. The couple had two sons: Jezreel, named for the city where Jehu killed Ahab's household, and Lo-ammi, whose name means "not my people." They also had a daughter, Lo-ruhamah, whose name means "no compassion." These little ones were so named to remind the Israelites of the cost of Israel's betrayal and that God would withhold compassion toward His people until they returned to Him. Hosea's wife, Gomer, also served as a symbol of Israel's betrayal. An unfaithful wife, she had abandoned her family to pursue other men. Likewise, Israel, the unfaithful nation, abandoned God for Baal. Eventually, Gomer returned to Hosea, and he welcomed her back with open arms. When those closest to us fail us, let's extend the same grace as Hosea extended to Gomer . . . and when we're unfaithful to God, let's repent and thank Him for His grace.

Hosea 2

"I will sow her for Myself in the land.
I will also have compassion on her who had not obtained compassion,
And I will say to those who were not My people,
'You are My people!'
And they will say, 'You are my God!'"   —Hosea 2:23

The descendants of God's ancient people now live all around
the globe. But one day, God will reunite His scattered people in
their land. Even though they turned their backs on Him, God
has promised to show grace to His people. He made an eternal
covenant with Abraham, and He intends to keep it. One day,
Israel will return to God, and He will welcome them with open
arms. They will be His people, and He will be their God. Just
as Hosea extended grace to Gomer and accepted her back, God
accepts all who turn to Him through faith in His Son. For those
of us who have put our trust in Jesus Christ, God has made us
His children. We can't do anything to diminish His love or over-
shadow His grace. Thank God that He loves us no matter how
many times we fail. Let's integrate gratitude for God's grace into
our everyday lives.

Hosea 3

Then the Lord said to me, "Go again, love a woman who is loved by
her husband, yet an adulteress, even as the Lord loves the sons of
Israel, though they turn to other gods and love raisin cakes."
                                                —Hosea 3:1

With Jeroboam in power, Israel enjoyed prosperity and ease.
But often, with affluence comes moral decline. As God's chosen
people climbed the mountain of fortune, they abandoned Him

and tumbled back down the mountainside. They left their heavenly Husband to engage in spiritual prostitution. God enlisted His prophet Hosea to woo back His people, so God arranged a marriage between Hosea and Gomer. Like every newlywed, Hosea looked forward to a bright future with his new wife. He dreamed of kids, a house, and love; but he had no idea how severe life's tempests would get. Gomer's eventual adultery and abandonment of her family broke Hosea's heart, but even so God told Hosea to renew his vows to his unfaithful wife. We don't see that kind of unconditional love very often in our society. When was the last time we loved someone with God-like, self-forgetful love? Who needs our unconditional love today?

Hosea 4

They will eat, but not have enough;
They will play the harlot, but not increase,
Because they have stopped giving heed to the LORD.   *—Hosea 4:10*

Most people are on the endless search for more — bigger houses, nicer cars, and fancier clothes. The desire to move up in status plagues our society. And it plagued Israel too. The Israelites looked for something or someone to fill the deep hole in their lives. They begged lifeless wooden statues for good crops and protection from their enemies. They even pursued sexual promiscuity to find intimacy with false gods. As a result, the things that used to satisfy them, no longer did. The Israelites forgot that contentment comes from an intimate relationship with the Lord and trusting His provision. What do we pursue to fill our hearts? Do we long to obtain bigger and better things? Or do we long for more intimacy with God? When we seek first to love and obey God, He will give us contentment and satisfaction in our work and in our relationships (Ecclesiastes 2:24).

Hosea 5

Therefore I am like a moth to Ephraim
And like rottenness to the house of Judah. —Hosea 5:12

In Hosea's time, from the king and the priests all the way down to the citizens, the Israelites had abandoned their heavenly Husband and had become prostitutes of worthless idols. But God didn't give up on them. He sent prophets, warnings, and enemy nations to judge His people. God had bound Himself to Israel by an unconditional covenant with Abraham, but He still expected them to lead righteous lives in obedience to Him. And they had failed. So, just as a moth destroys beautiful clothing and rottenness ruins delicious food, God brought destructive judgments on His people. When Israel hit rock bottom, He wanted them to look up and see Him. Today, when Christians stray from God, the Holy Spirit convicts us of sin. Though the Lord is full of grace, His loving discipline reminds us that He expects obedience.

Hosea 6

And as raiders wait for a man,
So a band of priests murder on the way to Shechem;
Surely they have committed crime. —Hosea 6:9

The religious leaders during Hosea's time had an identity crisis. Though their character and chaste living should have reflected the Lord's holiness, Israel's priests committed capital crimes on the way to Shechem. The city of Shechem was a religious center in Israel as well as a cit`y of refuge, which provided safe harbor for those who had unintentionally committed crimes (Joshua 20:1–2, 7). But the priests had turned this city that represented God's grace into one characterized by aggression and sin. Though we don't commit capital crimes on the way to church, do we gossip about others or verbally slay our spouses and kids on our way to worship God? In James 3:11–12, the apostle posed a question that can help us evaluate our lives: *Can fresh and salty water come from the same stream?* Our speech and the resulting actions reveal the contents of our hearts. If bitter words flow from our mouths, our hearts must be bitter too.

Hosea 7

For their hearts are like an oven
As they approach their plotting;
Their anger smolders all night,
In the morning it burns like a flaming fire. —Hosea 7:6

Anger and wickedness smoldered in the hearts of Israel's princes and flared into a forest fire of murder plots. During Hosea's lifetime, God's people endured the assassinations of four kings: Zechariah, Shallum, Pekahiah, and Pekah (2 Kings 15:10, 14, 25, 30). Israel didn't realize that by killing their leaders, they had made themselves like a ship lost at sea. Their anger had caused them to self-destruct. Does anger smolder in our hearts, ready to flare up at any time? Anger itself isn't a sin, but it can lead to sin. If anger has become our way of life, we should confess our anger to the Lord and ask His help in dealing with the root cause, perhaps through the guidance of a Christian counselor or trusted church leader. Rage, if not dealt with, will flare up in sinful thoughts and actions, burning others sapping our joy, and destroying the quality of our lives.

Hosea 8

They have set up kings, but not by Me;
They have appointed princes, but I did not know it.   *—Hosea 8:4*

The Israelites acted like they were in charge. When it came to selecting the political leaders of their nation, they chose kings and princes according to who they thought would meet their needs and champion their policies. They forgot that God had selected Israel as His chosen people through whom God intended to display His glory and sovereignty. Israel's political leaders were to be God's representatives chosen by Him, but Israel didn't even pray for guidance when they voted. Sometimes, like the ancient Israelites, Christians forget to seek God's guidance. How many decisions, small or large, do we make without consulting God? Sometimes we divide our lives into sacred and secular realms and forget to pray about "secular" endeavors—like patience while driving in traffic or wisdom when voting. Have we compartmentalized our lives and pushed the sovereign Lord into the "spiritual" compartment? Have we forgotten that God cares about our every decision and every thought?

Hosea 9

I found Israel like grapes in the wilderness;
I saw your forefathers as the earliest fruit on the fig tree in its first
   season.
But they came to Baal-peor and devoted themselves to shame,
And they became as detestable as that which they loved.
              —Hosea 9:10

Love is powerful. It drives us to sacrifice ourselves for the sake of another. We want to spend time with the one we love. Eventually, we even start to look like the object of our devotion. God had chosen the people of Israel and promised to care for them. The Lord loved His people, but they loved false gods. Israel devoted itself to Baal and followed all the detestable rituals that Baal worship required. Eventually, Israel started to look detestable just like Baal. As Christians, how we spend our time, energy, and money shows what we love. If we want to look more like Jesus and grow in our love for Him, we *must* spend time with Him daily, read God's Word, and share our lives with Jesus' followers. There's no shortcut to Christlikeness. Have we created the margin in our lives to spend the time we need with Christ so that eventually we will look like Him?

Hosea 10

Sow with a view to righteousness,
Reap in accordance with kindness;
Break up your fallow ground,
For it is time to seek the LORD
Until He comes to rain righteousness on you.   —Hosea 10:12

When a farmer wants to make his land productive, he clears it. He then takes his plow and tills the hard earth to allow oxygen and sunlight to penetrate below the surface. Then he scatters seeds, diligently waters them, and waits for harvest. Israel, however, produced spiritual crops of wickedness and, in return, was about to reap God's judgment. Through Hosea, the Lord pled with His people to break up the hard soil of their hearts by repenting from sin and following His Law. God wants to break up the hard soil of our hearts so He can make us spiritually productive.

Unfortunately, when He sets His hand to the plow and goes to work on us, it hurts. Sometimes the Lord allows loneliness or restlessness to soften us, and other times it takes tragedy and pain. But when God overturns our lives and His light penetrates the dark places, He will begin to work through us.

Hosea 11

Yet it is I who taught Ephraim to walk,
I took them in My arms;
But they did not know that I healed them. —*Hosea 11:3*

God chose Israel out of all the nations on earth. In His sovereignty, God decided that He would tell the world about His grace, holiness, and justice through a small, seemingly insignificant group of people. The Lord delivered them from Egyptian slavery, and in return they made themselves slaves to idols. Just as a loving father teaches his toddler to walk, the Lord taught the Israelites how to walk with Him. In return, they ran away from Him and sought protection from other nations. God led them with love by giving them the Law and teaching them righteousness. In return, they followed the path of injustice and wickedness. Today, God displays His image and demonstrates His grace through the church. But how will the world see God's love and justice if the church doesn't live with integrity? And how will our culture learn about God's grace if we don't meet our communities' spiritual and physical needs?

Hosea 12

Even the LORD, the God of hosts,
The LORD is His name."   — *Hosea 12:5*

After Jacob deceived his brother Esau and fled his wrath, Jacob collapsed exhausted at Bethel. As he slept, he dreamed of a staircase connecting heaven and earth, with angels ascending and descending it and with the Lord standing above it. At Bethel, the Lord confirmed to Jacob the covenant He had made to Abraham, and He promised to always be with Jacob and with all His people. But God's people had forgotten His covenant and His memorial name — *the* LORD, the self-sufficient Sovereign who commands angelic armies and deserves worship. Through Hosea, the Lord called His people to turn to Him just as Jacob had turned from his deceitful ways and trusted God at Bethel. Have we forgotten God's memorial name? Do we acknowledge the Lord's sovereignty in our lives — in joys, tragedies, and monotony? If we disregard God's providence and fail to remember His presence with us, we're in danger of drifting away from Him.

Hosea 13

Yet I have been the LORD your God
Since the land of Egypt;
And you were not to know any god except Me,
For there is no savior besides Me.   — *Hosea 13:4*

God's people had seen a river flow with blood and frogs and locusts overtake the land, and they had walked between walls of water into freedom. But the Israelites had soon forgotten these miraculous events that had led their nation to establish its sovereignty in the Promised Land. By Hosea's day, God's people had forgotten their special status as His chosen people. They had neglected His grace and had become experts at sin. Anyone who has experienced God's deliverance—whether from drugs, disease, loneliness, and so on—wants to give his or her life to God out of gratitude. But over time, we tend to forget what the Lord has delivered us from and that His Son is our *only* Savior. Let's not be like the Israelites who experienced God's deliverance from Egypt and then completely forgot Him. Whether our testimonies are dramatic or ordinary, God has saved us from judgment, and for this we should dedicate our lives to Him every day.

Hosea 14

Whoever is wise, let him understand these things;
Whoever is discerning, let him know them.
For the ways of the Lord are right,
And the righteous will walk in them,
But transgressors will stumble in them.   *—Hosea 14:9*

Our society doesn't suffer from a lack of intelligence. Many parents begin grooming their toddlers for college and pressuring their teens to attain advanced degrees. But intelligence doesn't equal wisdom. A wise person acknowledges not only God's existence but His intimate knowledge of all people, a knowledge that pierces to the deepest places in our souls. Discerning men and women consider the results of their actions beforehand. The wise care about what God thinks. At the end of his message to God's rebellious people, Hosea concluded with an application: wise people don't trip over the Lord's righteous laws. If we find that we get easily tripped up by obeying God's ethical standards or we find that the ways of the world have become increasingly appealing, we should pause. True wisdom requires us to read God's Word with the goal of practical application, not merely intellectual stimulation.

Joel

Joel 1

To You, O LORD, I cry;
For fire has devoured the pastures of the wilderness
And the flame has burned up all the trees of the field.
Even the beasts of the field pant for You;
For the water brooks are dried up
And fire has devoured the pastures of the wilderness.

—Joel 1:19–20

In the book of Joel, the prophet described an unrelenting locust plague that had ripped through Judah. Everyone — clergy, farmer, and wine-bibber included — was challenged to fast and prepare a solemn assembly, because the prophet knew that God had used the plague to chasten His people (Deuteronomy 28:21). The land itself and the wild animals had been in a state of groaning, but the people of Judah did not know how to petition the Lord without Joel's leading. The Galveston Hurricane of 1900. The Dust Bowl of the 1930s. Hurricane Katrina in 2005. These natural disasters devastated the United States' economy, forced people into hunger and homelessness, and cost thousands of lives. Survivors were left in the midst of devastation and trauma. Although the Lord no longer uses natural disasters to punish His people, we still experience the groans and pangs of a fallen world through these natural events. Earth and all that is in it await complete healing.

Joel 2

*The L*ORD *utters His voice before His army;*
Surely His camp is very great,
For strong is he who carries out His word.
*The day of the L*ORD *is indeed great and very awesome,*
And who can endure it?
*"Yet even now," declares the L*ORD*,*
"Return to Me with all your heart,
And with fasting, weeping and mourning;
And rend your heart and not your garments."
*Now return to the L*ORD *your God,*
For He is gracious and compassionate,
Slow to anger, abounding in lovingkindness
And relenting of evil.   —*Joel 2:11–13*

Have you ever asked children to apologize for their bad behavior? With arms folded and eyes narrowed in anger, they whisper the most insincere apologies. Judah's inhabitants had yet to apologize sincerely to the Lord for their spiritual infidelity, even after the locust plague. As a result, the Lord was preparing a foreign army to invade Judah. Joel entreated infants, newlyweds, *everyone* to humble themselves and ask the Lord to spare them. As Joel described to the people the severity of the invasion, God interrupted Joel with this message for His people: *Wait, Joel . . . tell them to return to Me. Tell them of My grace and compassion.* God isn't enthusiastic about disciplining His children. The perfect Father, He desires a sincere apology, a tender heart, and a break with bad behavior. While some earthly parents may reject the sincere apology from a child, God is *always, always* a refuge for confession. He not only hears confession, He blesses it.

Joel 3

The LORD roars from Zion
And utters His voice from Jerusalem,
And the heavens and the earth tremble.
But the LORD is a refuge for His people
And a stronghold to the sons of Israel.   —Joel 3:16

We have seen despots rule with corruption and murder, madmen who traffic children, and zealots who mercilessly oppress women. Does God care? Will He do something? Experiencing injustice can lead us into despair. Joel's prophecy reassured a hopeless people that God *did* see and vengeance is His (Romans 12:19). Even though the Lord is slow to anger and abounding in loving-kindness (Joel 2:13), there is a time when judgment is inevitable for the unrepentant. On the other side of the day of judgment, there is lasting peace for the people of God. One day, the mountains of Zion will drip with sweet wine, and the hills will flow with milk (3:18). God will justly judge, and peace will prevail. Here lies our hope: those who put their trust in God need not fear in the day of trouble. God was, is, and always will be a refuge for His people.

Amos

Amos 1

Thus says the LORD,
"For three transgressions of Edom and for four
I will not revoke its punishment,
Because he pursued his brother with the sword,
While he stifled his compassion;
His anger also tore continually,
And he maintained his fury forever.
So I will send fire upon Teman
And it will consume the citadels of Bozrah." —Amos 1:11–12

Because the Lord is holy, His judgment falls on everyone guilty of sin — this is true for both Jews and Gentiles. Amos, whose name is Hebrew for "burden bearer," had the duty of formally pronouncing judgment primarily to the northern kingdom of Israel. In Amos' prophecy, the Lord is the authority figure condemning His vassals for their failure to adhere to a covenant of understanding. Suzerain-vassal treaties — benevolent agreements between a powerful king and subordinate kings of other nations — were common in the ancient Near East. There were stipulations to the treaties, with dire consequences for insubordination. The legal rhetoric of "for three transgressions and for four" demonstrates the extent of each nation's violation of moral law, thereby legally justifying God's righteous punishment toward these violator nations. The Lord enacted poetic justice specific to the nature of each nation's crimes. As you frustrated with injustice? Take your frustrations to God. He sees injustice, and He hears your prayers.

Amos 2

Thus says the LORD,
"For three transgressions of Israel and for four
I will not revoke its punishment,
Because they sell the righteous for money
And the needy for a pair of sandals.
These who pant after the very dust of the earth on the head of the
*   helpless*
Also turn aside the way of the humble;
And a man and his father resort to the same girl
In order to profane My holy name.
On garments taken as pledges they stretch out beside every altar,
And in the house of their God they drink the wine of those who have
*   been fined."*   —*Amos 2:6–8*

The kingdom of Israel had strayed far afield, even with its privileged access to the God who brought them out of Egypt and into the Promised Land. With detail, God listed Israel's failings—a list more extensive than any other nation's (including its sister kingdom, Judah). Israel's special status as God's people did not exempt them from God's punishment. Israel took for granted the love and protection of God and lived in unrepentant rebellion, flagrantly punishing God's prophets, worshiping false gods, and plundering the poor. What was true in Old Testament days is true in ours: our status as Christians isn't a VIP pass; mature Christians don't just kick back and wait for heaven. We represent our Father. We help the weak because it's "more blessed to give than to receive" (Acts 20:35). We bring the gospel to the spiritually needy, because we know that without God's grace, we would still be in need ourselves (Ephesians 2:1–2).

Amos 3

Surely the Lord God does nothing
Unless He reveals His secret counsel
To His servants the prophets.
A lion has roared! Who will not fear?
The Lord God has spoken! Who can but prophesy? —Amos 3:7–8

Although the words of God were a violent roar, as was the case in the majority of prophecies, His growling pronouncements of judgment also served as caution. There is grace in the growl—within the pronouncement is also an opportunity for the people of God to repent. The kingdom of Israel was given fair warning. The nation had an opportunity to repent as the people of Nineveh did when Jonah reluctantly prophesied to them (Jonah 3:5–10). In Nineveh's case, amazingly, the Lord relented from His wrath. But how did the Israelites respond to Amos' prophecy? Unfortunately, they chose the path of denial. Who knows what would have happened if the people of the northern kingdom had humbled themselves and turned from their wicked ways? Their obstinacy can serve as a lesson to us: heed the gracious warnings that the Lord is faithful and kind to offer. Heed them, and repent.

Amos 4

"I overthrew you, as God overthrew Sodom and Gomorrah,
And you were like a firebrand snatched from a blaze;
Yet you have not returned to Me," declares the LORD.
"Therefore thus I will do to you, O Israel;
Because I will do this to you,
Prepare to meet your God, O Israel."   —*Amos 4:11–12*

Blighted crops, conquered cities, drought, and war: these terrible circumstances were *sent* by God to the Israelites. He took no joy in causing His children to suffer, but the Lord is true to His word. In Deuteronomy 28, the Lord set before the people of Israel a list of blessings and cursing. The people would be blessed as a result of their faithful obedience, and they would be cursed as a result of their idolatry and disobedience. God recounted the signs of cursing that the Israelites *should* have recognized (Amos 4:6–11). They had wandered so far from God's statutes that they didn't know when to say "uncle!" Sometimes we are in dire circumstances as a result of living in a world in desperate need of redemption. But other times, our plight is the result of our own foul choices. In either case, the Lord desires that we look to Him for help. But God is not mocked—He wants us to acknowledge our weakness and rely on His strength to carry us through.

Amos 5

"I hate, I reject your festivals,
Nor do I delight in your solemn assemblies.
Even though you offer up to Me burnt offerings and your grain
      offerings,
I will not accept them;
And I will not even look at the peace offerings of your fatlings.
Take away from Me the noise of your songs;
I will not even listen to the sound of your harps.
But let justice roll down like waters
And righteousness like an ever-flowing stream."   *—Amos 5:21–24*

God's dirge, or funeral song, was an indictment against the injustice of the nation of Israel. The unfaithful Israelites traveled on pilgrimages to religious sites for show, all the while accepting bribes and charging the poor just to have a judicial hearing. God's measure of righteousness is how His people treat those who are the most vulnerable in society—those who are poor or foreign or bereaved. Still, even as the Lord sang His dirge over the people, He shared His love for them, urging them to seek Him and the good so that they might live (Amos 5:6, 14). God is not impressed by the size of our church buildings or budgets or how much wealth we accumulate. He wants first place. That's it. God wants primary devotion and influence in our lives, so that *He* is glorified through whatever resources He blesses us with. It's only when we surrender our all to Him that we can truly live in abundance.

Amos 6

Woe to those who are at ease in Zion
And to those who feel secure in the mountain of Samaria,
The distinguished men of the foremost of nations,
To whom the house of Israel comes.
Go over to Calneh and look,
And go from there to Hamath the great,
Then go down to Gath of the Philistines.
Are they better than these kingdoms,
Or is their territory greater than yours?   *—Amos 6:1–2*

In Amos' day, the people of Israel gave in to greed, living in opulence and bragging about the territories they conquered—as if it were not God who blessed them with all they had. The cities with which God compared Israel—Calneh, Hamath, and Gath—are unfamiliar today because they were conquered and then faded into obscurity. God pointed to these cities, which were at one time larger and more prosperous than Israel. Then He pointed to Samaria, the capital of the northern kingdom, and essentially said, "You're next!" All too often, we choose to boast about our possessions and accomplishments as if we earned them in our own strength. In Paul's first letter to Timothy, he warned Timothy to flee from the love of money and run toward godliness (1 Timothy 6:10–11). God alone is the source of our prosperity and our shield from destruction. Why boast in anything or anyone but Him?

Amos 7

Then Amaziah, the priest of Bethel, sent word to Jeroboam king of Israel, saying, "Amos has conspired against you in the midst of the house of Israel; the land is unable to endure all his words."

—Amos 7:10

Sharing God's truth with God's people is no easy task. Amos, a shepherd by trade, found himself accused of treason by a priest. This confusion—where priests led the people into idolatry and could not discern God's words—enraged God. Amaziah the priest lost his family to violence and was taken captive because he led so many of God's people away from the sobering words they desperately needed to hear. Imagine if a scandal were stirred up in our country when a sheep farmer began to preach condemnation and the most influential preacher tried to quiet him and send him away. Who would we believe—the priest or the farmer? If we want to know whether a leader is serving God or himself, we must listen closely to how he handles God's Word. Does he avoid it? Does he study it? Does he teach from the Bible regularly?

Amos 8

Thus the Lord GOD showed me, and behold, there was a basket of summer fruit. He said, "What do you see, Amos?" And I said, "A basket of summer fruit." Then the LORD said to me, "The end has come for My people Israel. I will spare them no longer."

—Amos 8:1–2

Just as summer fruit came at the end of Israel's harvest, the time of provision and plenty was coming to an end. God had provided for Israel, but Israel had failed to mirror God's love by providing for the needy (Amos 8:4). God would bring spiritual famine (8:11) in response to Israel's willful ignorance; prophets would no longer speak. Though the people would long to hear from God, He would remain silent. This prophecy was fulfilled during the intertestamental period, when prophesying ceased between the time of Malachi's last prophetic utterance and the time of Jesus' birth. Mercifully, even during that period of pro- phetic silence, God had already provided His people with the Law, Wisdom Books, Historical Books, and the Prophets. Because the Lord has given believers two gifts—the completed canon of the Bible and the Holy Spirit who indwells and teaches us—we *never* have to suffer the agony of God's silence. Read the Bible as if God wrote it for you.

Amos 9

"Also I will restore the captivity of My people Israel,
And they will rebuild the ruined cities and live in them;
They will also plant vineyards and drink their wine,
And make gardens and eat their fruit.
I will also plant them on their land,
And they will not again be rooted out from their land
Which I have given them,"
*Says the L*ORD *your God.* —Amos 9:14–15

There is light at the end of the tunnel. There is hope even in the midst of discipline. In His grace, the Lord concluded Amos' prophecy not with condemnation but with hope. The first eight verses of chapter 9 emphasize God's ubiquitous presence wher- ever the people of Israel might try to flee. For Israel, there was no escaping God, whether in heaven or on earth or under the earth. And God still is a relentless pursuer of justice, and He will exact punishment on the unrepentant. However, we can be thankful God pursues His people in love with as much fervor as He pursues His people in justice. His mercy is fierce, and His compassion is dogged. Paul wrote of God's relentless pursuit in love: "For I am convinced that neither death, nor life, nor angels, nor principalities, nor things present, nor things to come, nor powers, nor height, nor depth, nor any other created thing, will be able to separate us from the love of God, which is in Christ Jesus our Lord" (Romans 8:38–39).

Obadiah

Obadiah

"The arrogance of your heart has deceived you,
You who live in the clefts of the rock,
In the loftiness of your dwelling place,
Who say in your heart,
'Who will bring me down to earth?'"   — *Obadiah 3*

The descendants of Esau enjoyed an almost impregnable position in the mountains southeast of the Dead Sea. Their geographical location gave them a military advantage along with a false sense of security, which God called "arrogance." This term comes from the Hebrew verb for "boiling"—used in the account of Esau squandering his birthright (Genesis 25:29, 34)—and refers to puffing up or inflating one's ego. Like the Edomites, we can resist God's control when our physical resources and blessings blind us to our need for Him. Such an attitude stems from an arrogance that deceives our hearts. Obadiah, the shortest book in the Old Testament, packs a wallop as the prophet urges us to remember that we have no security, safety, or reason for confidence apart from God. Humility allows us to trust in God alone for protection and provision.

Jonah

Jonah 1

But Jonah rose up to flee to Tarshish from the presence of the Lord.
So he went down to Joppa, found a ship which was going to Tarshish,
paid the fare and went down into it to go with them to Tarshish from
the presence of the Lord.   *—Jonah 1:3*

We often reduce Jonah's witness to cute children's stories and songs about being in the belly of a big fish, but what would cause Jonah to reject God's command and flee to Tarshish? Jonah's heading to Nineveh—an Assyrian city—to warn them would be like a World War II Allied soldier heading into Nazi Germany to warn them of coming wrath. Unlike other prophets, Jonah didn't prophesy to his own people but to the enemy! The tempest in Jonah's heart is demonstrated in the narrative: he kept "going down"—to Joppa, to the ship, to the hold of the ship . . . while God kept "hurling" back—with a great wind, with the jettisoning of the cargo, and finally, with Jonah being thrown into the sea. As believers, we are called to pray for those who use us and to love our enemies (Matthew 5:44). To demonstrate compassion toward our enemies may send us running in the other direction, but God, because He cares for our character, will hurl us back to exercise grace instead.

Jonah 2

"But I will sacrifice to You
With the voice of thanksgiving.
That which I have vowed I will pay.
Salvation is from the Lord."   *—Jonah 2:9*

When did Jonah feel inspired to pray to the Lord? In the depths of the sea, in the bowels of a fish, in the darkness, surrounded by half-digested sea creatures. Jonah's seemingly hopeless circumstances made him acutely aware of his helplessness, and he cried out in prayer and vows—thankful he had not been drowned. (Perhaps he took a lesson from the seamen of chapter 1 who cried out to God and were delivered from the storm.) Jonah wasn't perfect; the previous chapter portrayed him as a rebel, but his response to affliction is an object lesson for us on how to react when we encounter trials. God is worthy of praise regardless of our circumstances. Though it may seem counterintuitive to praise God during trials, it is a mark of Christian maturity (James 1:2–4). God hears our prayers and our praises. In Jonah's case, God's response came in the form of liberation from the fish, a second chance at obedience and life itself.

Jonah 3

When God saw their deeds, that they turned from their wicked way, then God relented concerning the calamity which He had declared He would bring upon them. —Jonah 3:10

Does anything burn your britches more than seeing a wicked person receive mercy? There is a reason for the viewing galleries at the gallows and witnesses to executions—people want to see the bad guys get what's coming to them. God asked Jonah a second time (what grace!) to prophesy to Nineveh. Jonah immediately did so, though he only prophesied to a portion of the city (Jonah 3:3–4). Then he perched on a nearby mountain to watch the calamity commence (4:5). In this case, though, the bad guys didn't arm themselves for battle. Nor did they dismiss the words of the Lord, as the Israelites did, despite many warnings. Instead, they fasted and repented and hoped in God's mercy. Do you see a theme here? The seamen of chapter 1, Jonah in chapter 2, and now the Ninevites in chapter 3 all cried out to God and hurled themselves at His merciful feet. Here's the revelation: we are *all* the bad guys. We all deserve death. "But God demonstrates His own love toward us, in that while we were yet sinners, Christ died for us" (Romans 5:8). *Mercy.*

Jonah 4

"Should I not have compassion on Nineveh, the great city in which there are more than 120,000 persons who do not know the difference between their right and left hand, as well as many animals?"
—*Jonah 4:11*

The book of Jonah ends with a question and leaves the audience—the people of God—to ponder the answer based on the pattern of the rest of the book. Should God *not* have compassion? Jonah was so resentful of God's lovingkindness toward Nineveh, he wanted to *die*. He wanted to see his enemies—men, women, children, and livestock—slain in the streets! Jonah cared more about his shade plant than he did about an entire city (Jonah 4:9). We are not far removed from Jonah's extremism: there are organizations and regimes that we would regard as beyond the mercy of God, when really, God's mercy extends much, much further than our limited compassion. If God's default is to be slow to anger and abundant in lovingkindness, if He relents from causing calamity (4:2), then shouldn't we imitate Him? We cannot follow God's example on our own strength., but because of the power of Jesus, we are able to starve our appetite for revenge and to love the unlovable, just as we who are unlovable have been loved by God (Romans 12:17–21; 1 Corinthians 6:9–11).

Micah

Micah 1

Tell it not in Gath,
Weep not at all.
At Beth-le-aphrah roll yourself in the dust. —Micah 1:10

On first reading, the opening chapter of the book of Micah would seem like a list of meaningless names and unrelated actions, but a little more information illuminates Micah's rhetorical skill. For example, "Tell it not in Gath, / Weep not at all. / At Beth-le-aphrah roll yourself in the dust" (Micah 1:10). The Hebrew text reveals more wordplay: "Gath" sounds similar to the verb for "tell it"; and rolling around in dust makes more sense as an imperative when the reader knows that "Beth-le-aphrah" means "house of dust." Micah's warnings were specific and by name. No matter how noble the name of the town, no one was immune from the specific scrutiny of God. Let's not regard people with famous names or fatter wallets as better than others. Instead, let's cultivate a knack for seeing the beauty and brokenness of each individual.

Micah 2

"If a man walking after wind and falsehood
Had told lies and said,
'I will speak out to you concerning wine and liquor,'
He would be spokesman to this people." —Micah 2:11

Good leaders tell it like it is; rather than resorting to people-pleasing, they discern what is true and lead people in the way that benefits those being led. Micah set out to tell God's truth to his neighbors—God's judgment was coming—at a time when his message was hardest to believe—a time of prosperity and decadence. Wealth was valued over integrity, and God's anger was especially focused on those who robbed the righteous just to have more. Micah's words cut against the grain of popular culture, and he certainly faced mockery and isolation for his faithfulness to God. Today, many leaders vie for the attention of God's people, but the litmus test for good leadership remains the same: if a leader strives to please God instead of people, the proof is in his or her discernment and courage to tell the truth rather than tickle ears and line their own pockets.

Micah 3

Thus says the LORD *concerning the prophets*
Who lead my people astray;
When they have something to bite with their teeth,
They cry, "Peace,"
But against him who puts nothing in their mouths
They declare holy war. —Micah 3:5

Israel's prophets and leaders in Micah's day were marked by greed and sensuality; their judgments and prophecies could be bought with a good meal. Yet, they still invoked the name of the Lord as the source of their authority. Even as these leaders sinned, they presumed that God's patience with them would never run out (Micah 3:11). This is the great risk of grace: there are always those who will abuse it. Paul wrote about this in Romans 6:15 when he asked, "What then? Shall we sin because we are not under law but under grace? May it never be!" May it never be that we who name the name of Jesus Christ are found on the side of selfish gain, abusing the grace God has given us. Instead, let us extend the grace we have freely received to others who desperately need it.

Micah 4

Many nations will come and say,
"Come and let us go up to the mountain of the LORD
And to the house of the God of Jacob." . . .
And He will judge between many peoples
And render decisions for mighty, distant nations.
Then they will hammer their swords into plowshares
And their spears into pruning hooks;
Nation will not lift up sword against nation,
And never again will they train for war.   —Micah 4:2–3

God had established Israel to be a kingdom of priests, a nation whose example would be a beacon of the righteousness and holiness of God to the nations. By Micah's time, the kingdom of Israel was far from godly, and its inhabitants chased the trappings and false gods of their neighbors. Captivity was coming; specifically the Babylonian captivity of the southern kingdom of Judah. Amazingly, Micah predicted the Babylonian captivity before Babylon was even a superpower. Assyria was the ruling empire at the time of his prophesying. Micah also wrote of a future time—the "last days"—when God's plans for Israel will come to fruition and the nations will converge on Mount Zion to inquire of the Lord. Hope is coming! We believers must cling to the promise that the day will come when we will "study war no more."

Micah 5

"But as for you, Bethlehem Ephrathah,
Too little to be among the clans of Judah,
From you One will go forth for Me to be ruler in Israel.
His goings forth are from long ago,
From the days of eternity."   —*Micah 5:2*

The Old and New Testaments are a masterwork of literary and historical unity. In Micah 5, we see foreshadowing of Jesus, our Messiah and Shepherd. Micah mentioned the birthplace of the Messiah—Bethlehem, the city of David—which indicated that the Messiah would be of David's family line. The verse also suggests the divinity of the Messiah, for only the divine could go forth from "the days of eternity" (Micah 5:2). Of course, Micah was not aware of Jesus. Matthew, in his account of the birth of Jesus, connected Micah's prophecy with Jesus as the Messiah (Matthew 2:3–6). Christians today are blessed to have the entire canon of Scripture serve as a witness to the King. We can be assured that this Shepherd-King will be our peace (Micah 5:5), He will restore Israel, and He will righteously reign in the millennium . . . and in eternity.

Micah 6

He has told you, O man, what is good;
*And what does the L*ORD *require of you*
But to do justice, to love kindness,
And to walk humbly with your God?   —*Micah 6:8*

The Lord did not delight in the endless offerings of rams and oil (Micah 6:7). Far more important to God than the sacrifice of many bulls and goats was a heart and soul inclined toward self-sacrifice and compassion, eager to act on behalf of justice, aware and caring for the marginalized. The stench of Israel's "wicked scales" of corruption (Micah 6:11) offended almighty God, because the scales represented the people's desire to satisfy only themselves. God's passion for sincere worship and simple compassion wasn't limited to the prophets or the Old Testament—it's a timeless truth. In Matthew 22:37–40, Jesus emphasized where believers ought to focus their efforts when He quoted Leviticus 19:18 and Deuteronomy 6:5: Love God with your all and love your neighbor as yourself. When we practice these things, we can be confident we are in the will of God.

Micah 7

Who is a God like You, who pardons iniquity
And passes over the rebellious act of the remnant of His possession?
He does not retain His anger forever,
Because He delights in unchanging love.   —Micah 7:18

This is the story of God's love for us: while we were yet sinners, Christ died for us (Romans 5:8). When Adam and Eve ate the forbidden fruit, God covered their nakedness (Genesis 3:21). Likewise, because of His compassion, God covered Israel with covenantal love, overlooking her shame (Ezekiel 16:8). We are just as hopelessly rebellious as the people of Israel were, but God *still* loves us and provides a way out for us. He passes over the stench of our sin and, with arms open, waits to receive us. Even when the people of Israel were unfaithful in their idolatry, God kept His word to bless Abraham and his descendants. God's loyal, steadfast love moved the apostle John to exclaim, "See how great a love the Father has bestowed on us, that we would be called children of God; and such we are" (1 John 3:1).

Nahum

Nahum 1

The LORD is good,
A stronghold in the day of trouble,
And He knows those who take refuge in Him.
But with an overflowing flood
He will make a complete end of its site,
And will pursue His enemies into darkness.   —*Nahum 1:7–8*

God gave Nahum the message that Jonah wished he could have preached one hundred years earlier: Nineveh *would* be destroyed. The short-lived repentance the Ninevites had shown to Jonah did nothing but delay the inevitable. The impending doom on Nineveh, the capital of the wicked Assyrian Empire, represented the justice God promises to mete out on all who refuse to repent and to believe in the Lord. On the other hand, the book of Nahum offers comfort to all of God's people "who take refuge in Him." Even though He may temper His timing with patience, God's justice will come with severity. In Nahum's day, as well as in ours — in times of unprecedented evil and of God's seeming absence — we can take comfort in knowing there will come a day when all believers will find satisfaction and all unbelievers will find condemnation under the scrutiny of God's impartial justice.

Nahum 2

For the LORD will restore the splendor of Jacob
Like the splendor of Israel,
Even though devastators have devastated them
And destroyed their vine branches.   —Nahum 2:2

Not only did God promise to destroy the Assyrians, those "devastators [who] devastated" His people in 722 BC, but the Lord also promised to restore the "splendor" of the Jews. The Hebrew term refers to an exaltation associated with authority and power, a prophecy Israel will realize only when the Messiah rules from Jerusalem in His millennial kingdom (Daniel 7:14–15). The "vine branches" destroyed by Nineveh will find restoration in the Messiah's reign, an era which prophecy characterizes as an age of abundant wine—and which Jesus foreshadowed in His first miracle (Genesis 49:11–12; John 2:1–11). As Christians, we also look forward to the time when we, along with Israel, will rule the world under the authority of the benevolent direction of Jesus Christ (Revelation 20:4–6). All the devastation of our lives will vanish in the light of Christ's glorious presence.

Nahum 3

"Behold, I am against you," declares the LORD of hosts;
"And I will lift up your skirts over your face,
And show to the nations your nakedness
And to the kingdoms your disgrace."   —Nahum 3:5

To lift up Nineveh's skirts represented an act of shame and divine retribution for the disgrace the nation had caused others. God would later give Babylon and even Jerusalem a similar message of judgment (Isaiah 47:1–3; Ezekiel 16:37). This message reveals that the Lord opposes *any* nation that thumbs its nose at His authority and disregards the value of human life. Even though Assyria's godless ways had endured for centuries, God devastated it when His sovereign purposes had run their course. The ruins of Nineveh stand as a warning to all countries that scoff at God's Word. The Lord unequivocally stated: "I am against you" (Nahum 2:13). On the other hand, God offers grace to any nation whose citizens see their wicked ways and repent (Jeremiah 18:7–8)—just as Nineveh did during the preaching of Jonah (Jonah 3:10).

Habakkuk

Habakkuk 1

"Look among the nations! Observe!
Be astonished! Wonder!
Because I am doing something in your days —
You would not believe if you were told." —Habakkuk 1:5

Habakkuk looked around at his rebellious nation of Judah and asked the Lord why He did nothing about it. How could the Almighty tolerate such evil? The prophet had a problem with God's inactivity. The Lord answered that He *was* doing something — in fact, something so astonishing Habakkuk wouldn't believe it even if God told him (Habakkuk 1:5)! The Lord planned to judge Judah's sin using a nation even more sinful than Judah. Now, Habakkuk had a problem with what God *was* doing. The cure seemed worse than the disease! God's sovereign plan is beyond finite human comprehension; He is under no obligation to reveal to us His ways. His will often remains a mystery to us because He is God, and we are not. However, if He chooses to reveal to us His plan, we might reject it and feel worse about God than we did before — all because of our limited understanding. For good reason, God told Habakkuk, "Observe! Be astonished! Wonder!" God's ways are so far above our ways, and His incomprehensible ways should cause us to worship Him — not to wander away from Him in doubt.

Habakkuk 2

"Though it tarries, wait for it;
For it will certainly come, it will not delay.
Behold, as for the proud one,
His soul is not right within him;
But the righteous will live by his faith."　　*—Habakkuk 2:3–4*

Wisely, Habakkuk took *to God* his concerns about God. The Lord assured the prophet that He would mete out justice in His time, and to "wait for it." In the meantime, in the seasons of confusion about God's ways and God's timing, how should God's people live? The Lord revealed two mind-sets people take with regard to God. The first reaction is pride—putting one's own will above the Lord's. The better response comes when the righteous person trusts God implicitly and "live[s] by his faith." So timeless and foundational is this principle, we find it repeated several times in the New Testament as the manner in which Christians are to live before God (Romans 1:17; Galatians 3:11; Hebrews 10:38). This type of faith begins at our salvation and extends into eternity.

Habakkuk 3

Though the fig tree should not blossom
And there be no fruit on the vines, . . .
Though the flock should be cut off from the fold
And there be no cattle in the stalls,
Yet I will exult in the LORD,
I will rejoice in the God of my salvation.　　*—Habakkuk 3:17–18*

At the end of the book, Habakkuk's attitude toward God had shifted. The prophet began with questions of accusation but changed to a posture of adoration. His words reflected no more understanding than he had at first. In fact, if anything, Habakkuk was more confused. But his response to God's timing and to His sovereign plans reflected a person who had chosen not to respond in pride but in faith. Many times in our lives we will find no figs on the tree and no cattle in the stalls. When we find ourselves questioning in pride what God is — or isn't — doing, we need to remember "the righteous will live by his faith" (Habakkuk 2:4). Peace comes as a result of faith — of believing that God remains in control and works all things for our good (Genesis 50:20; Romans 8:28).

Zephaniah

Zephaniah 1

Be silent before the Lord GOD!
For the day of the LORD is near,
For the LORD has prepared a sacrifice,
He has consecrated His guests. —*Zephaniah 1:7*

Zephaniah declared prophecies like edicts, with authority and force — perhaps because he was the descendant of King Hezekiah (Zephaniah 1:1). He prophesied in no uncertain terms "the word of the LORD" to the people of Judah: "I will cut off man from the face of the earth" (1:3). The Lord named false gods — Baal, the host of heaven, and Milcom — and called out priests who were guilty of idolatry. The Lord's punishment of the unfaithful, also known as the Day of the Lord, will usher in universal judgment. Zephaniah warned that God is coming not only for those who actively sin against Him by worshiping false gods, but He is coming also for those who do not come to Him for counsel (1:6) or for those who display indifference (1:12). Just as the Lord seeks worshipers who will worship Him in spirit and in truth (John 4:23), He also observes those of His own who are neither cold nor hot in their faith (Revelation 3:15). God is worthy of vibrant faith, which can only be achieved through dependence on Him. Any other religious display is disastrous.

Zephaniah 2

This is the exultant city
Which dwells securely,
Who says in her heart,
"I am, and there is no one besides me."
How she has become a desolation,
A resting place for beasts!
Everyone who passes by her will hiss
And wave his hand in contempt.   *—Zephaniah 2:15*

The Bible is clear: God resists, opposes, and punishes the prideful. (See Psalm 31:23; 94:1–2; Proverbs 15:25; 16:5; and James 4:6.) Pride is an effective tool in the hand of the Enemy, because the arrogance that often accompanies pride blinds its victims to their sure judgment. Such was the case with Nineveh, a pagan metropolis whose inhabitants were lost in their own self-importance. Despite an earlier revival when God's mercy saved the city as a result of Jonah's reluctant prophetic ministry, Ninevah's later generations forgot about God. Assyria (of which Nineveh was part) attacked the northern kingdom of Israel and carted away most of the nation's inhabitants to harsh exile. God had used the Assyrians as a tool of chastisement, but He had not forgotten the suffering of His people. Our lesson as believers is to cultivate a heart where pride can't grow. We must confess our sins and be accountable to others—not to avoid God's wrath but to be more like Christ.

Zephaniah 3

"For then I will give to the peoples purified lips,
That all of them may call on the name of the LORD,
To serve Him shoulder to shoulder.
From beyond the rivers of Ethiopia
My worshipers, My dispersed ones,
Will bring My offerings."   *—Zephaniah 3:9–10*

God established the nation of Israel as a people set apart — dedicated to the worship of God — through whom all nations would be blessed (Genesis 26:4). Through Israel, the world would come to know God and worship Him. Tragically, rather than serving as God's beacon, the nation of Israel mirrored its pagan neighbors, reflecting the wanton sin of surrounding cultures and willfully snubbing the Lord. Their disobedience, however, did not change God's compassionate vision for the nations. Zephaniah prophesied about the days that follow judgment, when every nation will worship the Lord "shoulder to shoulder" (Zephaniah 3:9). God's vision for every nation and tribe extended to the founding of the church in the book of Acts (Acts 1:8) and culminates in the eschatological vision depicted in Revelation 7:9. There is no nation that exists beyond God's gracious hand. As followers of Christ, we are called to be beacons to all nations.

Haggai

Haggai 1

"Is it time for you yourselves to dwell in your paneled houses while this house lies desolate?" Now therefore, thus says the LORD of hosts, "Consider your ways!"

—*Haggai 1:4 – 5*

The Jewish exiles who returned to the Promised Land began rebuilding the fallen temple of the Lord. But harassment from the locals and the Persians produced apathy toward the project — and the work stopped. After sixteen years without progress, God raised up the prophet Haggai to ignite in God's people a passion for God's priorities. Then, as now, it always seems easier to find time for improvements around the house than to make time for serving God's kingdom. Good intentions accomplish nothing without good works, and putting off biblical priorities until a better time is a carrot-and-stick approach to progress. We never catch the carrot. Why? For after today's distractions disappear, tomorrow has a new set of "good reasons" waiting to keep us from putting first things first. Our circumstances will never prove favorable to our priorities; it takes a choice. As Jesus said, "Seek first His kingdom and His righteousness, and all these things will be added to you" (Matthew 6:33). For the believer, living our priorities remains an act of faith. We trust God for our needs.

Haggai 2

" 'I will shake all the nations; and they will come with the wealth of all nations, and I will fill this house with glory. . . . The latter glory of this house will be greater than the former,' says the LORD of hosts."
—*Haggai 2:7, 9*

Some of the elderly among the Jews had seen the former glory of Solomon's temple, and they wept because the new temple the Jews were building paled in comparison. But Haggai urged the leaders and the people to "take courage . . . and work" (Haggai 2:4) to rebuild the Lord's temple. One day, God told them, the glory of the future temple will outshine even Solomon's: "The latter glory of this house will be greater than the former." The book of Hebrews quotes this context from Haggai about God "shaking" the nations and contrasts them with the kingdom we will receive when Jesus Christ rules the earth: "a kingdom which cannot be shaken" (Hebrews 12:28). As in Haggai's day, so we also look forward to the latter glory of Jesus' magnificent kingdom. Until then, "let us show gratitude, by which we may offer to God an acceptable service with reverence and awe" (12:28).

Zechariah

Zechariah 1

*Then the angel of the LORD said, "O LORD of hosts, how long will You
have no compassion for Jerusalem and the cities of Judah, with which
You have been indignant these seventy years?" The LORD answered
the angel who was speaking with me with gracious words, comforting
words.* —Zechariah 1:12–13

The Hebrew word for "Zechariah" is translated "the Lord remem-
bers." In the first chapter, the angel of the Lord asked the Lord
when He would show compassion to Judah. The Lord, in His
response of grace and comfort, proved that He did indeed remember His people. This sentiment of hope characterizes the book of
Zechariah: hope for the future of the people of Judah, hope for
the Messiah to come, and hope for the Day of the Lord—a final,
restorative day. Though God's message of hope was ill-received
by His people, and after the rejection, persecution, and murder
of His prophets, the Lord *still* chose to send the message of hope
to the world, through His Son, Jesus (Matthew 21:33–39). We
as believers are the recipients of God's relentless grace. May this
inspire us to share the good news with dogged compassion.

Zechariah 2

*"Many nations will join themselves to the LORD in that day and will
become My people. Then I will dwell in your midst, and you will
know that the LORD of hosts has sent Me to you.* —Zechariah 2:11

God's love is no respecter of persons. Though He has a special
purpose for the people of Israel, His desire is to be glorified
among the nations. One never needs to ask whether God's love
extends to Iraq or Timbuktu, New York or London—because

the answer, in Jesus Christ, is always a resounding yes! A veil of sin separates humanity from God, just as it did on the fateful day when Adam and Eve ate forbidden fruit and chose their own will over obedience to God. Yet, God desires to honor us with His presence. When Jesus became flesh and dwelt among people in the Holy Land, this scene was partially fulfilled. In the *eschaton*—the time in which all remaining prophecies are fulfilled, judgment is cast, and faith is made sight—God will once again dwell with humankind in redeemed eternity. In the present, believers have the presence of the Holy Spirit and the ministry of the church. Let's submit to being used of God to bring others into His presence.

Zechariah 3

Now Joshua was clothed with filthy garments and standing before the angel. He spoke and said to those who were standing before him, saying, "Remove the filthy garments from him." Again he said to him, "See, I have taken your iniquity away from you and will clothe you with festal robes." —Zechariah 3:3–4

The high priest, Joshua, was the subject of Zechariah's vision. He is mentioned numerous times in the Old Testament as one who helped rebuild the temple (Ezra 3:2). Joshua's role in the restoration of Israel was symbolic and pivotal. Symbolic, because Joshua—signifying the Israelite exiles—was unclean (the passage speaks of his being covered in excrement!) and therefore unworthy of representing God. Joshua's role was pivotal because he had been chosen by God for the role of high priest in spite of his uncleanliness. Joshua, whose name in Hebrew means "YHWH saves," typified the Branch (Zechariah 3:8), the righteous servant of God. "Branch" is also a preincarnate messianic reference to Jesus. All the while, at Joshua's side was the adversary, Satan, accusing Joshua. Our stories of redemption mirror Joshua's: detestable in our sin, accused by the Enemy, we would be condemned if not for the compassion of God through Jesus. Because He cleanses us from unrighteousness, we can be Jesus' representatives.

Zechariah 4

Then he said to me, "This is the word of the LORD to Zerubbabel saying, 'Not by might nor by power, but by My Spirit,' says the LORD of hosts." —*Zechariah 4:6*

Remember when our mothers hoisted us up to "assist" in changing a light bulb or our dads recruited us to help mow the lawn with our bubble mowers? The results were a brighter room and a manicured lawn, but even more than that, we experienced a sense of community and shared experience. Such is the work of God . . . He desires us to take part in His mission, He equips us to participate, and He energizes us toward the task. The post-exile returnees of Zechariah's day faced a formidable undertaking in rebuilding the land that God gave them. How would they get it done? Not by their power, but by the enablement of the Lord. In a world where affluence, corruption, and bullying are the rule, we can be confident in God's exceptional ability to cause us to persevere and participate according to His will.

Zechariah 5

Then he said to me, "This is the curse that is going forth over the face of the whole land; surely everyone who steals will be purged away according to the writing on one side, and everyone who swears will be purged away according to the writing on the other side. I will make it go forth," declares the LORD of hosts, "and it will enter the house of the thief and the house of the one who swears falsely by My name; and it will spend the night within that house and consume it with its timber and stones."

—Zechariah 5:3–4

Communion with God requires holiness. God cannot commune with sin. Purging sin was a necessary part of restoring the community of Israel to Himself. First came the conviction of the Word: anyone who dealt dishonestly with his neighbor by stealing or with God by falsely swearing would be convicted by the scroll (Zechariah 5:4). Then, wickedness would be banished (5:11). To be clear: it's impossible to live in this fallen world with this ontological sin nature and *not* sin. That's why God's cleansing and restoring was essential for the exiles and is essential for believers today. However, a lifestyle of unrepentant sinfulness and a casual indifference to profanity toward God has no place in His community. Be encouraged, though! The Holy Spirit indwells the Christian! The Holy Spirit is God's pledge, an inheritance of sensitivity to God's will, conviction of sin, and comfort in trials (John 14:26; 16:7–11; Ephesians 2:13–14). Through the Holy Spirit, we can commune confidently with God.

Zechariah 6

*"Then say to him, 'Thus says the L*ORD *of hosts, "Behold, a man whose name is Branch, for He will branch out from where He is; and He will build the temple of the L*ORD*. Yes, it is He who will build the temple of the L*ORD*, and He who will bear the honor and sit and rule on His throne. Thus, He will be a priest on His throne, and the counsel of peace will be between the two offices."'"*

—Zechariah 6:12 – 13

Wars, injustice, famine, disenfranchisement, corrupt leadership, lascivious living. It doesn't end here — the Branch is coming. God commissioned Joshua to rebuild the Lord's temple. But that's not all — God also *crowned* him to portend a future ruler: a messianic priest and king who would "sprout up from His place" (Zechariah 6:12 NET) — language similar to Isaiah 11:1 and Isaiah 53:2 — and build God's incorruptible temple. The writer of Hebrews expressed how Jesus fulfills the priest-king role of Messiah:

> For it was fitting for us to have such a high priest, holy, innocent, undefiled, separated from sinners and exalted above the heavens; who does not need daily, like those high priests, to offer up sacrifices, first for His own sins and then for the sins of the people, because this He did once for all when He offered up Himself. For the Law appoints men as high priests who are weak, but the word of the oath, which came after the Law, appoints a Son, made perfect forever. (Hebrews 7:26 – 28)

As believers, we must rest in the truth that war, injustice, and sin have an expiration date, and the compassionate holy rule of the Son will reign forever.

Zechariah 7

"Thus has the Lord of hosts said, 'Dispense true justice and practice kindness and compassion each to his brother; and do not oppress the widow or the orphan, the stranger or the poor; and do not devise evil in your hearts against one another.'" —*Zechariah 7:9–10*

James 1:27 reads, "Pure and undefiled religion in the sight of our God and Father is this: to visit orphans and widows in their distress, and to keep oneself unstained by the world." James may have been reading Zechariah 7 before he wrote under inspiration of the Lord! God made clear that He is unimpressed with outward demonstrations of piety. Empty rituals did not and do not curry favor with God, and fasting for show, which Jesus warned His disciples against in Matthew 6:16–18, is useless. Happily, God is direct in explaining the way to His heart: love the vulnerable—the poor, the widowed, the orphan, the foreigner—and stand up for justice. God says to "practice" kindness—to constantly be about the business of considering the needs of others. Whenever we care for the most vulnerable in our circles, we can be confident that we are serving in the will of God.

Zechariah 8

*"Thus says the L*ORD *of hosts, 'If it is too difficult in the sight of the remnant of this people in those days, will it also be too difficult in My sight?' declares the L*ORD *of hosts."* —*Zechariah 8:6*

"The LORD of hosts" is the name of God the prophet Zechariah used most—53 times in 14 chapters and 18 times in this chapter alone. Another way to translate the name is "the LORD over all," which speaks to the boundless power of God in the midst of impossible circumstances. The former exiles needed more than a pep talk to begin the daunting work of rebuilding the temple—they needed to hear time and time again that the Lord of hosts would be their strength in the face of challenge. The Lord of hosts is also with believers today in the face of persecution, financial difficulty, sickness, relationship woes, and even during those dark nights of the soul when He feels so far away. The Lord over all is sovereign, capable, compassionate, and never surprised by circumstances. Nothing is too difficult for Him.

Zechariah 9

Rejoice greatly, O daughter of Zion!
Shout in triumph, O daughter of Jerusalem!
Behold, your king is coming to you;
He is just and endowed with salvation,
Humble, and mounted on a donkey,
Even on a colt, the foal of a donkey.
I will cut off the chariot from Ephraim
And the horse from Jerusalem;
And the bow of war will be cut off.
And He will speak peace to the nations;
And His dominion will be from sea to sea,
And from the River to the ends of the earth.   *—Zechariah 9:9–10*

One way a consumer knows that the product he or she buys is dependable is when it comes with a guarantee. The manufacturer is so confident of the product's dependability that it is declared to be built to last, not just for a couple of weeks but for a lifetime. Zechariah 9 is the best prophetic "guarantee" of Jesus' triumphal entry into Jerusalem as well as His coming reign in the millennial kingdom. Because Jesus did indeed ride on the foal of a donkey and received a king's welcome (Matthew 21:5; John 12:15)—just as Zechariah foretold—guarantees that the second part of Zechariah's prophecy—the time of peace to the nations and Jesus' dominion from sea to sea—will come to pass. Though we live in the great pause between Zechariah 9:9 and 9:10, we can take the accuracy of the already fulfilled prophecy as a guarantee that the rest, and the best, is yet to come.

Zechariah 10

Ask rain from the LORD at the time of the spring rain —
The LORD who makes the storm clouds;
And He will give them showers of rain, vegetation in the field to each
   man.
For the teraphim speak iniquity,
And the diviners see lying visions
And tell false dreams;
They comfort in vain.
Therefore the people wander like sheep,
They are afflicted, because there is no shepherd.

— Zechariah 10:1 – 2

Before and even during the exilic period, the people of Israel wandered from God and sought protection and blessing from false gods and diviners. The "teraphim" — or household idols — cropped up several times in the history of Israel. Rachel stole Laban's teraphim to protect her and Jacob (Genesis 31:19, 34 – 35). Michal deceived her father Saul by placing a life-sized teraphim in David's bed (1 Samuel 19:11 – 13). Like a lucky rabbit's foot or a special coin, the people of Israel held on to their false gods for help and protection. In Zechariah 10, God reminded His people that He alone rains down favor and causes prosperity. God, and God alone, is the giver of every good gift (James 1:17). Today, we don't need to waste our time with talismans; we can trust the One who rules over all to be our all-sufficient guide.

Zechariah 11

Then the LORD said to me, "Throw it to the potter, that magnificent price at which I was valued by them." So I took the thirty shekels of silver and threw them to the potter in the house of the LORD.
—Zechariah 11:13

Thirty pieces of silver—the same amount of money paid to Judas for betraying Jesus (Matthew 26:14–15)—was the symbolic severance paid to the Good Shepherd, depicted by Zechariah, for His faithful tending of the neediest of the victimized flock. It was paltry compensation for the Shepherd's service—an offensive payment. In Zechariah's symbolism, the people of Israel seriously undervalued the sacrifice of salvation and care given by God. In Jesus' day, the chief priests, who should have known best the attributes of the Good Shepherd, instead sought to put a contract out on Jesus for a paltry sum. To this day, we still undervalue Jesus, our Good Shepherd when we are stingy in our giving and, even worse, in our faith in His ability to direct our daily lives. We honor the Good Shepherd with our time, resources, and faith. We honor Him when we repent and recognize our need to be tended to in our state of brokenness. We honor Him with our gratitude.

Zechariah 12

"I will pour out on the house of David and on the inhabitants of Jerusalem, the Spirit of grace and of supplication, so that they will look on Me whom they have pierced; and they will mourn for Him, as one mourns for an only son, and they will weep bitterly over Him like the bitter weeping over a firstborn." —Zechariah 12:10

Zechariah 12:10 represents the beautiful confluence of history and prophecy, a demonstration of compassion and favor—because the Lord Himself would grant the Spirit of grace and supplication that His people would need in order to be sensitive to their own sin—and also the conviction that would lead each person to mourn the One whom they pierced. The conviction would no doubt remind the people of Israel of the Egyptians' cries for their firstborn, when the Lord was faithful in delivering His people from Egypt. God had spared their firstborn then, but centuries later He would not spare His own Son. Zechariah prophesied concerning the Savior's piercing (John 19:34) and the Jewish people's remorse at Pentecost (Acts 2:37). Finally, in the end times, the nation of Israel will be compelled to believe and mourn over Jesus, convicted that He died for them. Christians can reflect on the Father's deep love for us—that He would give His Son to save wretches like us. What love! What grace!

Zechariah 13

"In that day a fountain will be opened for the house of David and for the inhabitants of Jerusalem, for sin and for impurity."

—Zechariah 13:1

In Zechariah 13, the prophet spoke of a future cleansing for the people of Israel. The source of this cleansing is *the* Fountain—Jesus Christ. The righteous will stand with God while false prophets cower in fear. But this righteousness is not without cost—Zechariah prophesied that the Shepherd (previously mentioned in Zechariah 11:4–7) would be slain, the people of Israel scattered, and only a remnant would remain faithful to God. This prophecy had a near fulfillment in the founding of the church when Jewish believers were scattered and persecuted after Jesus' death and resurrection. The ultimate fulfillment of Zechariah's prophecy will be during the tribulation period when a remnant of the people of Israel will profess faith in Christ and after the tribulation live under His millennial rule. Next to the crystal clear purity of God's truth, false prophecies lose their potency. Let's be sure to quench our thirst for security and hope only through the living water of Jesus and regard all false doctrine as poison.

Zechariah 14

Then it will come about that any who are left of all the nations that went against Jerusalem will go up from year to year to worship the King, the LORD of hosts, and to celebrate the Feast of Booths.

—Zechariah 14:16

The exiles must have trembled when they heard the conclusion of Zechariah's prophecy: in the eschatological future, the Lord would be the King after causing the nations to lay siege to

Jerusalem and tromp it in military might. God would win the battle. Jerusalem would be safe, and every nation would bring tribute to the Lord during the Feast of Booths (or Tabernacles) during the millennial kingdom. The Feast of Booths is an eight-day celebration commemorating the Israelites' forty-year wandering in the wilderness, where God provided for the people of Israel between their exodus from Egypt and their entrance into the Promised Land. The holiday is joyful, and even foreigners are welcome to join in the festivities. Acts 1:11–12 foretells that Jesus, as the conquering King (Revelation 19:11–16), will return to the Mount of Olives (Zechariah 14:4) to battle for His people. We live in the in-between—after the resurrection but before the end times. But isn't it good to know the end of the story? God wins. He gets the glory. We don't need to wait—we can glorify Him even now.

Malachi

Malachi 1

"But when you present the blind for sacrifice, is it not evil? And when you present the lame and sick, is it not evil? Why not offer it to your governor? Would he be pleased with you? Or would he receive you kindly?" says the LORD of hosts. — *Malachi 1:8*

Imagine that the President of the United States accepted an invitation to an average citizen's dinner party. Would the hostess order pizza or give him a burger and fries or serve him leftover meatloaf? Of course not! But that's what God's priests were doing. The Mosaic Law outlined the kind of sacrifices God would accept — pure, spotless animals (Leviticus 22:18–20). The holy Lord deserves only the best. But the priests in Malachi's time offered God their leftovers. They laid injured, worthless animals on the altar and expected God's blessing. Though Christians today don't have to abide by the Mosaic Law, God expects us to sacrifice the very best of our resources, gifts, and time, and even our very selves to Him (Romans 12:1–2). Do we offer Him our dreams, plans, and loved ones, entrusting them to His providence? After all, God offered as a sacrifice His very best Lamb, His Son Jesus, for us.

Malachi 2

"For the lips of a priest should preserve knowledge, and men should seek instruction from his mouth; for he is the messenger of the LORD of hosts." — *Malachi 2:7*

God gave His priests the job to mediate between Him and His people. The Lord expected His priests to explain His Law and to challenge Israel to live by faith. The priests should have led by example, practicing spiritual disciplines that caused the roots of their faith to sink deep into their hearts and minds. In short, God's priests, who represented Him to God's people, were to take Him seriously. But they didn't. And neither did Israel. Pastors today should challenge Christians and dive below the surface of shallow Christianity. But lay people don't get off the hook either. All Christians must take responsibility for their spiritual growth. Are we just checking off the tasks on our spiritual to-do list, or are we growing? When Christians stop taking their relationship with God seriously, life becomes spiritual drudgery and worship loses its meaning. Christians can fall into religious ritualism just like the Jews in Malachi's day.

Malachi 3

"But who can endure the day of His coming? And who can stand when He appears? For He is like a refiner's fire and like fullers' soap." —Malachi 3:2

Slavery. Ponzi schemes. Religious persecution. Genocide. We don't have to look very far to find evil and injustice in our world. Likewise, when the Lord looked at the priests in Malachi's day, He saw idolatry, sexual immorality, exploitation, murder, and all kinds of wickedness. The people had no fear of God in their hearts, and as a result, they ran wild. So God spoke through His prophet Malachi, warning Israel about the coming judgment day. Messiah's coming would initiate cleansing among God's people, just as a refiner's fire removes impurities from metal and a fuller's soap scrubs away deep stains. When Jesus came the first time, He initiated a period of grace. And we are still in that period in which people can turn to God. Until Christ's coming when we will all bow before Jesus, the Holy Spirit continually refines Christians so that we better reflect Jesus' holiness.

Malachi 4

"But for you who fear My name, the sun of righteousness will rise with healing in its wings; and you will go forth and skip about like calves from the stall."　　　　　　　　　　　*— Malachi 4:2*

God's people needed healing. Their sin had resulted in God's judgment. For seventy years they had lived as captives in a foreign land and had finally returned and rebuilt their ruined cities. By Malachi's day, however, the memory of judgment had faded, and God's people once again practiced all the wicked deeds that had landed them in captivity in Babylon. The Jews needed God's restorative touch. God's people had chosen to walk in sin and darkness, but life was about to get darker. After Malachi's ministry, God's silence fell on His people for four hundred years — until a baby's cry pierced the dark silence. When Messiah came, His ministry displayed shalom — spiritual, physical, and relational health. Jesus came to lift up the poor, to free those bound by sin, and to heal the broken (Luke 4:17–21). Christians resemble their Savior most when they pursue spiritual, emotional, and relational healing in their families and communities.

How to Begin a Relationship with God

The Prophetic Books of the Bible describe the catastrophic consequences that awaited God's people because of their infidelity to the one true God. These books also share the heartbreak of a just *and* loving God: One who warns before the wrath and who grants His people the will to choose Him. The prophets' warnings still hold lessons for us today. They narrate the fallenness and inadequacy of humanity and the mercy of God in *always* providing a way out. God still seeks repentance over wrath; He continues to be quick to forgive and slow to punish. The Way, the Truth, and the Life, Jesus Christ, offers us sure and permanent peace with God. If you are reading this and do not yet know Jesus, I implore you to read on. Scripture reveals four essential truths we must all accept and apply to receive the life-transforming help God promises. Let's look at these four truths in detail.

Our Spiritual Condition: Totally Depraved

The first truth is rather personal. One look in the mirror of Scripture, and our human condition becomes painfully clear:

> "There is none righteous, not even one;
> There is none who understands,
> There is none who seeks for God;
> All have turned aside, together they have
>   become useless;
> There is none who does good,
> There is not even one." (Romans 3:10–12)

We are all sinners through and through — totally depraved. Now, that doesn't mean we've committed every atrocity known to humankind. We're not as *bad* as we can be, just as *bad off* as we can be. Sin colors all our thoughts, motives, words, and actions.

If you've been around a while, you likely already believe it. Look around. Everything around us bears the smudge marks of our sinful nature. Despite our best efforts to create a perfect world, crime statistics continue to soar, divorce rates keep climbing, and families keep crumbling.

Something has gone terribly wrong in our society and in ourselves — something deadly. Contrary to how the world would repackage it, "me-first" living doesn't equal rugged individuality and freedom; it equals death. As Paul said in his letter to the Romans, "The wages of sin is death" (Romans 6:23) — our spiritual and physical death that comes from God's righteous judgment of our sin, along with all of the emotional and practical effects of this separation that we experience on a daily basis. This brings us to the second marker: God's character.

God's Character: Infinitely Holy

How can God judge us for a sinful state we were born into? Our total depravity is only half the answer. The other half is God's infinite holiness.

The fact that we know things are not as they should be points us to a standard of goodness beyond ourselves. Our sense of injustice in life on this side of eternity implies a perfect standard of justice beyond our reality. That standard and source is God Himself. And God's standard of holiness contrasts starkly with our sinful condition.

Scripture says that "God is Light, and in Him there is no darkness at all" (1 John 1:5). God is absolutely holy—which creates a problem for us. If He is so pure, how can we who are so impure relate to Him?

Perhaps we could try being better people, try to tilt the balance in favor of our good deeds, or seek out methods for self-improvement. Throughout history, people have attempted to live up to God's standard by keeping the Ten Commandments or living by their own code of ethics. Unfortunately, no one can come close to satisfying the demands of God's law. Romans 3:20 says, "By the works of the Law no flesh will be justified in His sight; for through the Law comes the knowledge of sin."

Our Need: A Substitute

So here we are, sinners by nature and sinners by choice, trying to pull ourselves up by our own bootstraps to attain a relationship with our holy Creator. But every time we try, we fall flat on our faces. We can't live a good enough life to make up for our sin, because God's standard isn't "good enough"—it's *perfection*. And we can't make amends for the offense our sin has created without dying for it.

Who can get us out of this mess?

If someone could live perfectly, honoring God's law, and would bear sin's death penalty for us—in our place—then we would be saved from our predicament. But is there such a person? Thankfully, yes!

Meet your substitute—*Jesus Christ*. He is the One who took death's place for you!

[God] made [Jesus Christ] who knew no
sin to be sin on our behalf, so that we might
become the righteousness of God in Him.
(2 Corinthians 5:21)

God's Provision: A Savior

God rescued us by sending His Son, Jesus, to die on the cross
for our sins (1 John 4:9–10). Jesus was fully human and fully
divine (John 1:1, 18), a truth that ensures His understanding of
our weaknesses, His power to forgive, and His ability to bridge
the gap between God and us (Romans 5:6–11). In short, we are
"justified as a gift by His grace through the redemption which
is in Christ Jesus" (Romans 3:24). Two words in this verse bear
further explanation: *justified* and *redemption.*

Justification is God's act of mercy, in which He declares righteous the believing sinners while we are still in our sinning state.
Justification doesn't mean that God *makes* us righteous, so that
we never sin again, rather that He *declares* us righteous — much
like a judge pardons a guilty criminal. Because Jesus took our
sin upon Himself and suffered our judgment on the cross, God
forgives our debt and proclaims us PARDONED.

Redemption is Christ's act of paying the complete price to
release us from sin's bondage. God sent His Son to bear His wrath
for all of our sins — past, present, and future (Romans 3:24–26;
2 Corinthians 5:21). In humble obedience, Christ willingly
endured the shame of the cross for our sake (Mark 10:45;
Romans 5:6–8; Philippians 2:8). Christ's death satisfied God's
righteous demands. He no longer holds our sins against us,
because His own Son paid the penalty for them. We are freed
from the slave market of sin, never to be enslaved again!

Placing Your Faith in Christ

These four truths describe how God has provided a way to Himself through Jesus Christ. Because the price has been paid in full by God, we must respond to His free gift of eternal life in total faith and confidence in Him to save us. We must step forward into the relationship with God that He has prepared for us—not by doing good works or by being a good person, but by coming to Him just as we are and accepting His justification and redemption by faith.

> For by grace you have been saved through faith;
> and that not of yourselves, it is the gift of God;
> not as a result of works, so that no one may
> boast. (Ephesians 2:8–9)

We accept God's gift of salvation simply by placing our faith in Christ alone for the forgiveness of our sins. Would you like to enter a relationship with your Creator by trusting in Christ as your Savior? If so, here's a simple prayer you can use to express your faith:

> *Dear God,*
>
> *I know that my sin has put a barrier between You and me. Thank You for sending Your Son, Jesus, to die in my place. I trust in Jesus alone to forgive my sins, and I accept His gift of eternal life. I ask Jesus to be my personal Savior and the Lord of my life. Thank You. In Jesus' name, amen.*

If you've prayed this prayer or one like it and you wish to find out more about knowing God and His plan for you in the Bible, contact us at Insight for Living Ministries. Our contact information is provided on the following pages.

We Are Here for You

If you desire to find out more about knowing God and His plan for you in the Bible, contact us. Insight for Living Ministries provides staff pastors who are available for free written correspondence or phone consultation. These seminary-trained and seasoned counselors have years of experience and are well-qualified guides for your spiritual journey.

Please feel welcome to contact your regional office by using the information below:

United States

Insight for Living Ministries
Biblical Counseling Department
Post Office Box 5000
Frisco, Texas 75034-0055
USA
972-473-5097 (Monday through Friday,
8:00 a.m.–5:00 p.m. central time)
www.insight.org/contactapastor

Canada

Insight for Living Canada
Biblical Counseling Department
PO Box 8 Stn A
Abbotsford BC V2T 6Z4
CANADA
1-800-663-7639
info@insightforliving.ca

Australia, New Zealand, and South Pacific

Insight for Living Australia
Pastoral Care
Post Office Box 443
Boronia, VIC 3155
AUSTRALIA
+61 3 9762 6613

United Kingdom and Europe

Insight for Living United Kingdom
Pastoral Care
PO Box 553
Dorking
RH4 9EU
UNITED KINGDOM
0800 787 9364
+44 1306 640156
www.insightforliving.org.uk

Resources for Probing Further

God doesn't want Christians to simply increase their knowledge about Him and His Word. Our heavenly Father wants His children to know Him more intimately and apply His Word more fully to our lives. A multitude of books exist that tell us what the Bible says, but finding resources to help us *apply* its principles to everyday life is a bit more challenging. So we have compiled a list of resources that won't just take up space in your bookcase — they will help you live out God's Word each day. Keep in mind as you read these books that we can't always endorse everything a writer or ministry says, so we encourage you to approach these and all other non-biblical resources with wisdom and discernment.

Arnold, Clinton E., and others, eds. *Zondervan Illustrated Bible Backgrounds Commentary*, 4 vols. Grand Rapids: Zondervan, 2002.

Grudem, Wayne, C. John Collins, and Thomas R. Schreiner, eds. *Understanding Scripture: An Overview of the Bible's Origin, Reliability, and Meaning*. Wheaton, Ill.: Crossway, 2012.

Insight for Living. *Insight's Bible Handbook: Practical Helps for Bible Study*. Plano, Tex.: IFL Publishing House, 2007.

Insight for Living. *Insight's Old Testament Handbook: A Practical Look at Each Book*. Plano, Tex.: IFL Publishing House, 2010.

Kaiser, Walter C., Jr. *The Old Testament Documents: Are They Reliable and Relevant?* Downers Grove, Ill.: IVP Academic, 2001.

Merrill, Eugene H. *Everlasting Dominion: A Theology of the Old Testament*. Nashville: Broadman & Holman, 2006.

Merrill, Eugene H. *Kingdom of Priests: A History of Old Testament Israel*. 2nd ed. Grand Rapids: Baker Academic, 2008.

Morgan, G. Campbell. *Life Applications from Every Chapter in the Bible*. Grand Rapids: Fleming H. Revell, 1994.

Walvoord, John F., and Roy B. Zuck, eds. *The Bible Knowledge Commentary: An Exposition of the Scriptures by Dallas Seminary Faculty, Old Testament Edition*. Wheaton, Ill.: Victor Books, 1986.

Wiersbe, Warren W. *The Wiersbe Bible Commentary: Old Testament*. Colorado Springs: David C. Cook, 2007.

Wiersbe, Warren W. *With the Word: The Chapter-by-Chapter Handbook*. Nashville: Thomas Nelson, 1991.

Ordering Information

If you would like to order additional copies of *Insight's Bible Application Guide: Isaiah–Malachi—A Life Lesson from Every Chapter* or other Insight for Living Ministries resources, please contact the office that serves you.

United States

Insight for Living Ministries
Post Office Box 5000
Frisco, Texas 75034-0055
USA
1-800-772-8888
(Monday through Friday, 7:00 a.m.–7:00 p.m. central time)
www.insight.org
www.insightworld.org

Canada

Insight for Living Canada
PO Box 8 Stn A
Abbotsford BC V2T 6Z4
CANADA
1-800-663-7639
www.insightforliving.ca

Australia, New Zealand, and South Pacific

Insight for Living Australia
Post Office Box 443
Boronia, VIC 3155
AUSTRALIA
+61 3 9762 6613
www.ifl.org.au

United Kingdom and Europe

Insight for Living United Kingdom
PO Box 553
Dorking
RH4 9EU
UNITED KINGDOM
0800 787 9364
+44 1306 640156
www.insightforliving.org.uk

Other International Locations

International constituents may contact the U.S. office through
our Web site (www.insightworld.org), mail queries, or by
calling +1-972-473-5136.